THREE STEPS FORWARD

TWO STEPS BACK

Perservering through Pressure

THREE STEPS FORWARD

TWO STEPS BACK

Perservering through Pressure

Charles R. Swindoll

WORD PUBLISHING
Nashville · London · Vancouver · Melbourne

Published in Nashville, Tennessee, by Word, Inc.

Printed in the United States of America.

Library of Congress Cataloging-in-Publication Data

Swindoll, Charles R.
   Three steps forward, two steps back / Charles R. Swindoll.—
   Expanded ed.
     p.   cm.
   Includes bibliographical references.
   ISBN 0-8499-4098-2
   1. Perseverance (Ethics) 2. Christian Life—1960 -   I. Title
   BV4647.P45S94   1997   90-31849
   248.4—dc20   CIP

Contents

Living in a pressure-cooker world is tough—I mean *really* tough! Especially in this "aspirin age" of ours.

People like you and me find themselves hanging dangerously heavy weights of anxiety on very thin threads of patience. Those threads frequently snap and need mending. Among the many who hang in there, stress reaches a peak every few days.

Competition requires high-level performance. "People demands" add to the pressure. Tempers flare. Stomachs turn. Ulcers bleed. Hearts break. Nerves unravel. Minds blow. Some drop out. Most tighten their grip and try to cope.

As a former pastor in a multiple-staff ministry, I frequently came into contact with people in crisis. Sometime back I decided to keep a record of actual situations brought to my attention within a thirty-six-hour time span—matters that required pastoral counsel or direction of some kind. Here is what I recorded:

- A mother and dad committed their teenager to a local psychiatric ward.

- A relative of a girl in our church took her own life.

- A fifteen-year marriage went up in smoke as the wife walked out. She is now living with another man.

- A young couple had their first child. She has Down's syndrome.

- A woman in her twenties is plagued with guilt and confusion because of an incestuous relationship with her father years ago.

- A young woman on a nearby Christian campus was raped and stabbed.

- A former minister is disillusioned. He has left the faith.

- A middle-aged husband and wife cannot communicate without screaming. Separation seems inevitable.

- An employer is embittered because his Christian employee cannot be trusted.

- A missionary wife who has returned to the States has suffered an emotional breakdown.

- Christian parents just discovered their son is a practicing homosexual.

And then I got in my car after a late meeting that night—and it wouldn't start!

That's only *one page* out of my journal. Multiply one day's crises by 365. Add financial strain, inflation, traffic jams, unemployment, unplanned pregnancies, failure at school, obesity, smog, surgery, loneliness, alcoholism, drugs, and death. Subtract the support of the family unit. Divide by dozens of different opinions . . . and you come up with a formula that has the makings of madness.

Block all avenues of escape and you have an enormous powder keg with a terribly short fuse. Even if you are a Christian . . . and love God intensely . . . and believe the Bible . . . and genuinely want to walk in obedience.

Introduction

It occurred to me that somebody needs to address "the other side" of the Christian life. If for no other reason than to uphold reality, Christians need to be told that difficulty and pressure are par for the course. No amount of biblical input or deeper-life conferences or supervictory seminars will remove our human struggles. God promises no bubble of protection, no guaranteed release from calamity. Ask guys like Job or Joseph or Daniel or Paul!

Or—if you prefer—just read this book. It dances to a different tune, I should warn you. Not much is said about sudden blessings or overnight success. But a lot is said about standing firm through tough days. You'll become acquainted with an ancient term that has almost faded away in this generation under the bright, dazzling lights of splashy, always-grinning, a-miracle-a-day spirituality—*perseverance.* I know of no better partner to dance with when you're doing the three-steps-forward, two-steps-back number.

My special thanks go to Mrs. Helen Peters for her invaluable secretarial assistance as she typed and retyped the manuscript without complaint during many a long night. And to Peter Gillquist of Thomas Nelson, who is to be commended for his splendid editing skills and determination to see this book get into print originally.

Little did I realize that God would use the writing of this book to effectively show me firsthand what perseverance is all about. I'm thankful for the lessons this project has taught me . . . even though there were days I was convinced it should be entitled *One Step Forward, Five Steps Back!*

Charles R. Swindoll
Dallas, Texas

1

Perseverance: Archaic Word of Relevance

I was a bit weary after the four-hour-plus flight from Los Angeles to Miami. The plane pulled up to the gate and the engines shut down. I sighed, grabbed my briefcase, and strolled out into the terminal.

I caught the eye of the one who was to pick me up, a man I have known for a number of years. We smiled, shook hands, and started toward the baggage claim area. As I looked into his eyes, I asked, "How are you doing?"

His response was candid. He lives in an administrative pressure cooker. As a Christian involved in higher education, he experiences the real world in large, daily doses. So I wasn't surprised when he answered, "How am I doing? Growing and learning!"

Then he quickly added, "I used to say, 'Great . . . fantastic!' every time somebody asked me that. You know, the super-positive, everything-is-terrific response. Not anymore, Chuck. I am growing and I am learning—but frankly, I'm not always on top doing *great!*"

Realistic Expectations

Growing and learning. That's the Christian life in a nutshell, isn't it? It seems to me that more of us in God's family ought to admit that there are more "growing and learning" days than "great and fantastic" days. And that's nothing to be ashamed of. Growing and learning are healthy, normal experiences. Both have to do with a process . . . and that process is sometimes painful, often slow, and occasionally downright awful! It's like taking three steps forward and two steps back.

Don't misunderstand. Jesus is still Lord. God is still good. The victory is still ours. Nevertheless, life is tough. It's not a Disneyland. Or a rose garden. Or a Cloud Nine delight complete with loud fireworks and big-time tingles. Or daily miracles that make our checkbooks balance and recharge our dead batteries. Such expectations are not only unrealistic, they are unbiblical.

Listen to the apostle Paul:

> We are afflicted in every way, but not crushed; perplexed, but not despairing; persecuted, but not forsaken; struck down, but not destroyed. (2 Cor. 4:8–9)

Now *that's* where it's at. And that is precisely what this book is all about: persevering *through* the afflictions, the crushings, the blasts of life . . . without despairing and giving up.

You should know, too, that I am fresh out of exaggerated clichés about the "abundant life." This is *not* your typical "just grin-and-say-praise-the-Lord" book. But I *am* genuinely excited about sharing how Jesus Christ will stay with you when you err or hurt deeply or feel misunderstood and want to quit.

You see, I am of the opinion that His abundance overshadows the low tides of our lives just as much as it does the bright and beautiful times of ecstatic joy. In fact, it is when the bottom drops out and we start feeling insecure that our Lord slips in the back door and delivers stability.

The Four Spiritual Flaws

Before we get into the meat of our discussion about a truly attainable spirituality, let us make clear what the Christian life is *not*. There are four rather common misconceptions about spirituality and Christian maturity that simply do not hold water. Warning: They might come as a surprise, maybe even a shock. So hang on.

Flaw 1: Because you are a Christian, all your problems are solved.
We do a great disservice to an unbeliever when we bait him by saying, "Come to Christ and all your problems will be over." The Bible never says that. It promises that we will be new creatures; it assures us that we will have a destiny that is secure; but it does not guarantee a downhill slide once Christ comes into a person's life. In fact, in some instances problems increase and the road gets rougher!

Flaw 2: All the problems you will ever have are addressed in the Bible.
They're not. It is very unwise for us to make broad, sweeping statements in areas where the Scriptures do not speak. There are many times when we don't find an explicit answer in Scripture for our particular problem. At such times we are forced to walk by faith, trusting the Lord to show us the next step as it is needed. The Bible simply does not offer a specific answer to every problem in life.

Flaw 3: If you are having problems, you are unspiritual.
Isn't it a shame that this idea is conveyed in so many places today? Having a problem simply proves you are human! We all have problems, and you're not unspiritual because you are

wrestling with a dilemma. As a matter of fact, some of the most spiritual men and woman I have ever known have wrestled with some of the deepest problems life offers.

Think of Job and his suffering. He did not have an answer. He did not understand why. His counselors, with their severe and heady statements, were grossly deceptive; they didn't know the answers either. Although Job was spiritual, he had enormous problems.

Flaw 4: Being exposed to sound Bible teaching automatically solves problems.

Bible instruction alone will not result in instant solutions to problems. No matter how reliable the teaching or how gifted the teacher, the declaration of truth does not provide the removal of difficulties.

Think of the Scriptures as an absolutely accurate map. A map tells you how to get to a certain destination. But just looking at a map won't automatically transport you to Arizona or England or Peru. Getting to those places means you have to make the effort . . . pay the cost . . . take the time for travel . . . stay at it until you arrive.

So it is in the Christian life. God's map is reliable and available. It is also clear and direct. But there is no hocus-pocus in its pages that automatically sends its reader by way of a magic carpet.

What Is Christian Maturity?

Anyone with a family of children has a built-in illustration of maturity. In the Swindoll family there are four kids—a boy on each end and two girls in the middle. Each one has a distinct personality, a unique set of characteristics that makes that person an individual.

But there was one thing equally true of all four—they grew up *fast*. They matured. They became increasingly more responsible, and they learned how to handle themselves correctly in everyday situations. As my wife, Cynthia, and I observed their growing maturity, we were delighted. Maturity is a joy to behold.

So it is in God's family. We are born into it by faith in the Lord Jesus Christ. At first, as spiritual babies, we are fragile, irresponsible, milk-drinking infants who lack discernment and strength. But as time passes, we should begin to grow up spiritually. As our Father observes our maturity, it pleases Him. He sees our resiliency, our responsibility, our enlarged diet, our increased discernment, our sensitivity to Him, and our strength—and it delights Him.

The theme of Hebrews 5:11–14 is maturity—and the lack of it. In verse 11, which speaks of an ancient priest, we read:

> Concerning him we have much to say, and it is hard to explain, since you have become dull of hearing.

It was not that the Hebrews hadn't heard; it was that they had not obeyed. They had heard sounds in their ears, but they had become hard of listening, dull of hearing. We read further:

> For though by this time you ought to be teachers, you have need again for someone to teach you the elementary principles of the oracles of God, and you have come to need milk and not solid food. For everyone who partakes only of

milk is not accustomed to the word of righteousness, for he is a babe. But solid food is for the mature, who because of practice have their senses trained to discern good and evil. (Heb. 5:12–14)

What is a sign of maturity? Practicing what you hear. Through practice you become mature. You see, it is one thing to grow *old* in the Lord, but it is another thing to grow *up* in the Lord.

There are many people cruising from church to church, from Bible conference to Bible conference, filling notebook after notebook, wearing out Bible after Bible, who are still some of the crankiest, fussiest, most irresponsible people you meet. Why? Because they do not practice the things they hear.

This is the whole thrust of the book of James. I call James the New Testament's "man from Missouri." He wants you to put to the test what you claim to believe—by doing it! A mature person is one who is involved in practicing on a regular, consistent basis what he hears and what he takes in. Just being exposed to Bible instruction won't solve problems.

Maturity is a process I like to call "spiritual osmosis." We hear and absorb biblical truth and then allow that truth to pervade our inner lives down deep where attitudes are formed and decisions are made. Then, as circumstances arise that call for a supernatural response, the indwelling Holy Spirit has sufficient ammunition to give us stability and power to cope. This works in all sorts of difficult experiences.

When irritations come, obey God and carry out His Word in dealing with them. When temptations come, apply principles of Scripture that help you face them victoriously. When the sins of the flesh arise, apply the truths you have been taught. It is in the experience of all this application that you become wise and more mature.

A person would be insane to hear his physician diagnose his ailment as a rapidly growing tumor, and then think that just because he had *talked* with his doctor, the growth would suddenly disappear. No, he's going to have to be operated on. Likewise, just being exposed to the truth won't make us mature. Nor will it alone—without application—solve *one* problem.

Please don't misunderstand. I love God's Word! I am more convinced than ever in my life that its trustworthy truths are of inestimable value. But although the Bible may be a trustworthy Book, it is certainly no magic potion that you rub on yourself three times a day to chase the devil away. Nor is it something you take internally with a pious promise to God, hoping that the next morning you will suddenly know and experience all its truths.

There is no such "instant maturity" available on this earth. God does not offer a formula that produces fully mature Christians overnight. Christian growth comes through hard-core, gutsy perseverance (a forgotten word!) of applying what you hear and obeying it . . . and thereby learning how to handle those inevitable problems.

My Miami friend is absolutely right. There are an enormous number of "growing and learning" days in comparison to the "great, fantastic" ones.

In this book I am going to isolate specific situations that we all face almost daily—or at least weekly—and address them from an aggressive, biblical stance. Understand that we are not trying to dodge our problems; instead, we are gearing up to confront our setbacks, walk *into* them, *through* them, and come out stronger in Christ. This book is filled with real world stuff. It will provide you with some helpful information that blends unsheltered, bottom-line reality with an understandable and attainable spirituality. In short, it is a book that is committed to helping you persevere through pressure.

PART I
External Pressures

2

Misunderstanding: Paralyzing Sting of Humanity

Few things are more difficult to live with than being misunderstood. Sometimes it's downright unbearable.

When you are misunderstood, you have no defense. And have you noticed that when you are misunderstood, no matter how hard you try to correct the misunderstanding, it usually gets worse? You go fully loaded, ready to "set them straight," and all you do is dig yourself deeper! The harder you work, the worse it gets and the deeper it hurts. Its sting can be paralyzing.

A close friend of mine has an acquaintance in Texas who is a young attorney. He is a member of a sizable law firm run by a rather traditional kind of boss who enjoys a special kind of ritual at Thanksgiving time. Every year this young attorney participates in the ritual because it means so much to his employer.

On the large walnut table in the boardroom of the office suite sits a row of turkeys, one for each member in the firm. It isn't just a matter of "if you want it, you can have it; if you don't, you can leave it." The members go through some rather involved protocol.

Each man stands back from the table and looks at his turkey. When his turn comes, he steps forward and picks up the bird, announcing how grateful he is to work for the firm and how thankful he is for the turkey this Thanksgiving.

This young attorney is single, lives alone, and has absolutely no use for a huge turkey. He has no idea how to fix it, and even if it were properly prepared he has no way to use all its meat. But because it is expected of him, he takes a turkey every year.

One year his close friends in the law office replaced his turkey with one made of papier-mâché. They weighted it with lead to make it feel genuine, and attached a real turkey neck and tail to make it look just like a real turkey. But it was a bogus bird through and through.

On the Wednesday before Thanksgiving, everyone gathered in the boardroom. When it came his turn, this young man stepped up, picked up the large bird, and announced his gratitude for the job and for the turkey.

Later that afternoon, he got on the bus to go home. With the big turkey on his lap, he wondered what in the world he would do with it. A little further down the bus line, a rather rundown, discouraged-looking man got on. The only vacant seat on the bus was the one next to our young attorney friend.

He sat down and they began to talk about the holiday. The lawyer learned that the stranger had spent the entire day job-hunting with no luck, that he had a large family, and that he was wondering what he would do about Thanksgiving tomorrow.

The attorney was struck with a brilliant idea: *This is my day for a good turn. I'll give him my turkey!*

Then he had a second thought. *This man is not a freeloader. He's no bum. It would probably injure his pride for me to give it to him. I'll sell it to him.*

He asked the man, "How much money do you have?"

"Oh, a couple of dollars and a few cents," the man answered.

The attorney said, "I would like to sell you this turkey." And he placed it on the man's lap.

"Sold!" The stranger handed over the two dollars and whatever coins he had. He was moved to tears, thrilled to death that his family would have a turkey for Thanksgiving. He got off the bus and waved good-bye to the attorney. "God bless you. Have a wonderful Thanksgiving. I'll never forget you." The bus pulled away from the curb, as both men smiled.

Can you picture this man going home, announcing as he got inside the front door, "Kids, you'll never believe what a nice man I met today! Come here, look what I have."

Then he'd lay the thing down, I'm sure, on the kitchen table and begin to unwrap the brown paper, only to find this fake glob of paper and lead weights, with only a real neck and real tail. What the man probably said, Simon and Schuster couldn't even publish!

The next Monday, the attorney went to work. His friends were dying to know about the turkey. You cannot imagine their chagrin when they heard the story of what happened. I understand, through my friend, that they all got on the bus every day that week looking in vain for a man who, as far as I know, to this day still entertains a misunderstanding about a guy who innocently sold him a fake turkey for a couple of bucks and a few cents.

That's misunderstanding!

Analyzing Misunderstanding

I don't think there is a person reading this who needs that awful feeling amplified. To one degree or another, we have all had that experience. When you stop to analyze it, there are two steps involved in misunderstanding. First, an innocent act or word or implication causes a misunderstanding. What makes it so painful is that you *innocently* say something or do something or imply something that is mistakenly interpreted. Second, an offense is created as a result.

My wife and I were misunderstood by a merchant in our city one time. We went shopping for a new dishwasher, found one we thought we liked, and said we wanted to think about it. He agreed to hold our check while we thought it over and decided. "Fine, no obligation, no problem," he said. We believed him.

It so happened that we changed our minds—which is a customer's prerogative (we thought!). So I went back into the store and said, "We've changed our minds and would like to have our check back." Well, he shared with me a piece of his mind that he couldn't afford to lose. He cursed and tore up the check into tiny pieces, strewing them on the floor. Remembering I was a minister, he began to give me the business (he was now yelling) about what was I as a preacher doing telling him how to run his business.

I was misunderstood!

And no matter how I tried, how loud I might have shouted back (which I did not, although I gave it serious thought), I was still misunderstood.

Now that kind of thing happens all the time—even to a Christian. You experience in your own little world a measure of what we could call persecution. And the persecution might come from an innocent act or word or implication. You didn't mean anything by it, but it was misread and an offense was created.

We're not alone. If it's any comfort to you, this has always been standard operating procedure for the people of God. It's part of the growing process. You do not grow fully and completely without sometimes being misunderstood.

Illustrating Misunderstanding

Let me show you a man in the Scriptures who was misunderstood. David had just finished killing the giant Goliath. Samuel had already anointed his head with oil and announced to the family of Jesse, "Your youngest is going to be king." But learning how to be king included learning how to endure being misunderstood.

Saul, the current king, was a very threatened, insecure man. If you've ever worked for a man like Saul, you understand what David faced. The slightest irritation created an enormous sense of insecurity for Saul.

David had slain the giant, and he and Saul were coming back from the Philistine war. As they entered the city, the women who had gathered sang a song they had written in honor of the victory.

> And it happened as they were coming, when David returned from killing the Philistine, that the women came out of all the cities of Israel, singing and dancing, to meet King Saul, with tambourines, with joy and with musical instruments. And the women sang as they played, and said, "Saul has slain his thousands, And David his ten thousands." (1 Sam. 18:6–7)

Oh, oh! It was not just the nine thousand difference that bothered Saul. It was the fact that David was getting the glory Saul wanted. And Saul misunderstood that "young whippersnapper" who had killed the giant innocently, just serving the Lord. Saul was thinking, *That David is out to get my job.*

Then Saul became very angry, for this saying displeased
him; and he said, "They have ascribed to David ten thousands, but to me they have ascribed thousands. Now what
more can he have but the kingdom?" (1 Sam. 18:8)

Notice the exaggeration! David wasn't looking for the
kingdom. He just woke up one morning and killed a giant.
That doesn't happen every day. And after killing the giant, he
was Saul's man; in fact, he became Saul's personal musician.
He was not out to get the throne for himself; that was by God's
appointment. But Saul, seeing not only David's courage but
now his popularity, misunderstood him. "And Saul looked at
David with suspicion from that day on" (1 Sam. 18:9).

An innocent and courageous act was incorrectly interpreted
so that deep down in Saul's heart, he was convinced that David
was out to get the throne.

Understanding Misunderstanding

Most Old Testament scholars believe that David's Psalm 140
was written as a result of the events we have just discussed. You
will realize, as you read the psalm, that David is on the run. He
has to be. He is being hunted and haunted by the madman
Saul. Being misunderstood is always uncomfortable, but being
misunderstood by Saul was miserable!

There is a sense in which we can approach an awareness of
how misunderstandings work—how they progress. For in
Psalm 140 we see a *pattern of development* that gives us some
much-needed wisdom to lean upon the next time we are misunderstood.

First of all, there is a sense of *vulnerability*. Notice verse 1: "Rescue me, O Lord," then "Preserve me" and "Keep me, O Lord" in verse 4. Those are the words of a vulnerable person. By *vulnerable* I mean being defenseless and unprotected. Vulnerability is the first expression of this misery. Being misunderstood invariably catches you off guard; you stumble into it inadvertently.

Then comes the next step: *exaggeration*. Remember how Saul, when he heard the women's song, said: "They're assigning those 'ten thousands' to David. What more can he want then but the kingdom?" When people misunderstand you, they add to it the exaggeration that has built up in their minds. Their imaginations run wild. Recall my appliance salesman?

Look how exaggeration affected David's enemies; they devised evil: "[They] devised evil things in their hearts; They continually stir up wars" (Ps. 140:2). Isn't that vivid!

When you are the object of a misunderstanding, you can see how the person who starts with just a *slight* misunderstanding gradually builds it up to the place where he or she begins to believe out-and-out lies about you.

Consider a jealous husband who, for a moment, entertains the thought concerning his wife, *I'm not sure I can trust her.* Perhaps she said she would be home at a certain time. When she comes in an hour and a half later, the husband says, "Where were you?" She gives a factual account of how she was detained— legitimately. He's not sure he believes it. He's suspicious. That fuels his imagination, and he begins to probe further with questions that are incredibly wild and uncalled for.

You may not believe it, but I know of a case where that exact situation happened. The next day the man began to check the odometer to see how far she was driving. He checked it in the morning, made his little notation, and then checked it again when he came home. She had driven, let's say, 6.4 miles.

He walked in and said, "Hi, honey. How are you?"

"Fine," she said.

He asked, "Where did you go today?"

She answered, "I went to the store."

"Which one did you go to?"

"Safeway."

"Safeway, huh? Where else did you go?"

"Nowhere."

"Oh, yes you did! It's only 2.1 miles to Safeway, but the odometer reads . . ."

What was he doing? He was imagining his way through a misunderstanding. Our fallen minds are like that. When we choose to misunderstand, we fuel the fire of exaggeration. And if you have ever been misunderstood, you know what I'm talking about. It gets worse, not better, as time passes. That's part of the sting of being misunderstood.

The third step comes in Psalm 140:3: "They sharpen their tongues as a serpent; poison of a viper is under their lips." People not only entertain misunderstanding in their hearts, but they share it and *speak it aloud.* They punctuate it in someone else's mind, who now says, "Oh, I never knew *that.* Why, it makes sense. And you know what else I heard?" Just to make it a bit more juicy, they'll add a little here, stretch it a tad there to make the story really sing. And before long, they're loving it.

Meanwhile, you sit alone at home. You're not praying; you're thinking, *O Lord, what else are they saying?* as you bite your nails right down to the knuckle.

Now you know why James says the tongue is an organ that can control us. David said, "Poison of a viper is under their lips."

I heard recently that no creature's tongue moves faster than a serpent's. They're sometimes called "treble-tongued" because their tongues move so fast that they actually look like three tongues at once. David knew what he was talking about.

Listen: The only muscle you need to break down another person's dignity is the muscle hidden inside your mouth. You can destroy a life with your tongue.

I read of a case in which a woman's suicide note simply read, "They said. . ." She never finished. Something "they said" killed her.

Overcoming Misunderstanding

You say, "What can I do when this sort of thing happens?" This is what David did: "I said to the Lord, 'Thou art my God'" (Ps. 140:6). Notice he *said* this to the Lord. I suggest that you *say* it, not just think it. We need to verbalize our allegiance to the living God. There are times I say to the Lord right out loud, "Lord, You are mine. I count on You right now." That's precisely what David did.

I remember that as I was growing up I had an intense desire to become a professional football player. And I had specific plans to grow up big! Now, I became somewhat large, but not quite like what I had in mind. I had fantasized about becoming this huge defensive end for the Green Bay Packers. I pictured myself with God hovering over me. Then when the Lord needed someone to get after bad people, He'd say, "Hey, take care of that guy for Me. Sic 'em!" And I would.

But as I actually grew up, I realized I would never have that sort of physical size or clout, so I learned to let God fight some of my battles. The techniques are decidedly different. Now, there are times I say, "Lord, take care of that person. I can't fight him. He's smarter than I am. He's been fighting longer. Besides, I'm weary. You do it."

And, you know, He does! I have seen Him do battle. It's like Ed "Too Tall" Jones fighting a dwarf. It's as though we have the right, when our enemies encompass us, to say to them, "Watch it, or I'll tell God on you!" In fact, just before the parting of the Red Sea in that dramatic escape from Pharaoh, General Moses encouraged his people by saying, "The Lord will fight for you while you keep silent!" (Exod. 14:14).

And David wrote:

Do not grant, O LORD, the desires of the wicked;
Do not promote his evil device, lest they be exalted.
(Ps. 140:8)

If that were not enough, look how David invited the Lord to finish off his enemies!

"As for the head of those who surround me,
May the mischief of their lips cover them.
May burning coals fall upon them;
May they be cast into the fire,
Into deep pits from which they cannot rise."(Ps. 140:9–10)

"Lord, put 'em in the pits." It's amazing what you find in the Bible!

Let me tell you, the person who coexists with misunderstanding and bitterness is miserable. These enemies will hound you, nipping at your heels. But when you give the situation over to God and say—"Lord, I am defenseless. I am misunderstood. I am right, but they'll never believe it. You take over"— God will perform the most unbelievable feats as He glorifies His name in your life. That's His specialty!

We *grow* through misunderstanding. Through it, we come to see the Lord as our defense. You can lie down at night knowing that although the tongue of your accuser might be wagging, God is taking care of that situation.

Do you have some "friend" at school giving you grief? Tell God about him! Is there some individual at work that you can't handle, no matter what you do? Look, that's why you have a Savior, a Deliverer. You were born into the *family* of God, so don't be content to live like an orphan. Learn to bring your misunderstandings to Him.

One summer my wife and I went through one of the most painful times of our lives. Disarmed and defenseless, we got a firsthand, bitter taste of that painfully familiar paralyzing sting of humanity. We had done what was right, but we were misinterpreted and therefore maligned. Unfair criticism increased the pain and brought us, in tears, to our knees. I remembered a statement C. S. Lewis once made:

> God whispers to us in our pleasures, speaks in our conscience, but shouts in our pains: it is His megaphone to rouse a deaf world.[1]

Believe me, He had our undivided attention! Crushed and bruised, all we could do was wait.

Although the swelling from that sting is now gone, the memory is not. We shall *never* forget those anguishing weeks. But now that they are past, something very beautiful has emerged in our lives. We are much more sensitive to others, much more concerned about putting ourselves in the other guy's shoes.

There's a lawyer in Texas who would give anything to convince one special family he's no turkey. But, alas, that probably will never happen. For some, the swelling never seems to go down.

3
Stress: Threatening Storm of Anxiety

One of my all-time favorite children's books is entitled *Alexander and the Terrible, Horrible, No Good, Very Bad Day.* This little kid named Alexander (probably not more than seven or eight years old) has "one of those days." I mean, nothing goes right. He has back-to-back disappointments and tragedies like you can't imagine. It's one continuous "downer." The dear little guy can't win for losing. Take, for example, when he awakes in the morning:

> I went to sleep with gum in my mouth and now there's gum in my hair and when I got out of bed this morning I tripped on the skateboard and by mistake I dropped my sweater in the sink while the water was running and I could tell it was going to be a terrible, horrible, no good, very bad day.[1]

After a terrible day at school, a horrible visit with the dentist, and a no-good stop at the shoe store, Alexander slumps in his chair at the supper table. His troubles continue:

> There was lima beans for dinner and I hate limas. There was kissing on TV and I hate kissing. My bath was too hot, I got soap in my eyes, my marble went down the drain, and I had to wear my railroad-train pajamas. I hate my railroad-train pajamas. When I went to bed Nick took back the pillow

he said I could keep and the Mickey Mouse night light burned out and I bit my tongue. The cat wants to sleep with Anthony, not with me. It has been a terrible, horrible, no good, very bad day.[2]

Small wonder that our little friend sighs at the end of a day like that and says, "I think I'll move to Australia."

Days like that prompt chapters like this. They create tension. They become oppressive, fretful, intense days of anxiety. *Stress* is the term I'll use in this chapter. We're all familiar with it.

Analysis of Stress

Humans are strange creatures. We run faster when we lose our way. Instead of pausing to regroup, we ricochet from place to place. Three words describe our times: hurry, worry, and bury.

In this race called life, when the pressing demands of time are upon us, we need to stop and get oriented. We need to discover that the Lord is God. He will be exalted; He is with us; He is our stronghold.

Remember during your growing-up years how your mother had a specially designated wall with some pencil marks on it where, as you grew from year to year, she marked where your head reached? We had such a wall in our home. (In fact, we ran out of ways to define which mark belonged to which child!) It was interesting to see how our children went through certain growth spurts at times.

On occasions, it was convicting when I came back from a trip and one of the smaller children asked, "Daddy, how much did *you* grow while you were away?" No, they didn't have spiritual growth in mind, but I often thought about their question in that light. They wanted to know, "Do you keep growing? When does it stop?"

God uses an infinite number of vehicles in the process of helping us grow. I do not know of any means that leads to *instant* growth. I've never met anyone who became instantly mature. It's a painstaking process that God takes us through, and it includes such things as waiting, failing, losing, and being misunderstood—each one calling for extra doses of perseverance. In your own spiritual growth, where are the marks on the wall of your life? Where do you stand in light of last year? Or how about the last decade?

Units of Stress

Dr. Thomas. H. Holmes and his colleagues at the University of Washington have done considerable research in the area of human stress. They measured stress in terms of "life-change units." On their scale, the death of a spouse rated 100 life-change units. Divorce from one's mate rated 73 units. Pregnancy rated 40; remodeling a home 25 . . . and Christmas rated 12 units (which isn't surprising!).[3]

Their conclusion was that from a strictly human viewpoint, no person in his own strength can handle 300 or more units in a 12-month period without suffering physically or emotionally within the next two years.

We are constantly faced with stress-producing situations—the death of a friend, a divorce in the family, loss of employment, the heartache brought on by a sick child, the news from a physician that there is some "question" in the X-ray.

I received a letter from a close friend not long ago. I was stunned to read the words that were written in a shaky long-hand. A certain stress had affected his family's whole lifestyle. My friend's wife had gone to the physician for her annual checkup. During the examination, the physician had discovered a mass of unexplained tissue in her breast. It had reached into the lymph areas, and there was a very strong possibility of malignancy.

Eminently successful in his work as a CPA with an international accounting firm and having an outstanding salary and track record, my friend has always made the grade—and then some—through college and right on into business. They are a marvelous Christian family. But suddenly—BOOM! The stress factor soared.

A Psalm for the Stressed

Psalm 46 was born in the context of severe stress. It's a balm for the stress-ridden. Martin Luther, who was under continual stress and even satanic opposition, in studying Psalm 46 saw that "God is our refuge and strength, a very present help in trouble." As a result, he wrote the hymn "A Mighty Fortress Is Our God." It was drawn from Psalm 46.

> God is our refuge and strength,
> A very present help in trouble.
> Therefore we will not fear, though the earth should change,
> And though the mountains slip into the heart of the sea;
> Though its waters roar and foam,
> Though the mountains quake at its swelling pride.

There is a river whose streams make glad the city of God,
The holy dwelling places of the Most High.
God is in the midst of her, she will not be moved;
God will help her when morning dawns.
The nations made an uproar, the kingdoms tottered;
He raised His voice, the earth melted.
The LORD of hosts is with us;
The God of Jacob is our stronghold.

Come, behold the works of the LORD,
Who has wrought desolations in the earth.
He makes wars to cease to the end of the earth;
He breaks the bow and cuts the spear in two;
He burns the chariots with fire.
"Cease striving and know that I am God;
I will be exalted among the nations, I will be exalted in the
    earth."

The LORD of hosts is with us;
The God of Jacob is our stronghold.

For me, the theme is in the first verse. If I could put it in a modern paraphrase, the words would read like this: *God is our instant help when we are in a tight squeeze.* That's what it says. The word *trouble* in the Hebrew means "to be restricted, to be tied up in a narrow, cramped place." There's an old Deep-South expression: "between a rock and a hard place." You've heard it; you've probably used it. That's exactly the spot the psalmist was in when he wrote Psalm 46!

Being between a rock and a hard place means I am being pressed. I'm being squeezed in; stress is doing a number on me.

Do you sense it too? The psalmist's message to us at those times is that God is a refuge and a strength. That's the theme. When you're pressed, when you're under stress, when you're pushed down and your weakness is displayed, God is building a tent of refuge. He's protecting you; He's surrounding you with His custodial care and strength.

Let's look at the overall view of the psalm. Three situations are revealed, and all three are extremely relevant to us.

The first is what I would call upheaval in nature (Ps. 46:1–3). When a natural phenomenon occurs that is threatening, it brings stress. And what is the reaction? Verse 2 says (let's make it personal): "I will not fear." The stress is an upheaval in nature, but the reaction is, "I'll stand fast."

Second is a civil disturbance (Ps. 46:4–7). The city is under attack. And the reaction? "God is in the midst of her, she will not be moved."

The third situation is what I call post-battle fatigue (Ps. 46:8–11). You will see the reaction in verse 10: "Cease striving and know that I am God." So, "I will not strive."

There are the natural phenomena that occur, bringing fear and threat. I will not *fear*. There is a city under attack. I will not be *moved*. There is a time following those awful experiences when fatigue or depression sets in. I will not *strive*. Why? "Because God is our refuge and strength, a very present help in trouble" (Ps. 46:1).

Conquering Fear

Let's take a closer look at these stress situations. Natural phenomena: "We will not fear, though the earth should change, and though the mountains slip into the heart of the sea [does that sound familiar to Californians?]; though its waters roar and foam, though the mountains quake at its swelling pride."

We who have lived in the western United States know what it is to experience mud slides when the rain won't stop. Or to feel the tremor of the earth when the San Andreas fault sort of nods in our direction and grimly says, "Remember, life is transitory."

Or how about when the hills dry out and fires sweep in? I was talking once to several acquaintances from Santa Barbara who were preserved from a devastating fire. They told the most incredible stories. These fires can sweep down through a canyon at thirty, forty, up to fifty miles an hour.

One family had a swimming pool, and their girls were in swimming. They saw the fire coming over the canyon. Almost before they could grab their towels and run, the fire was upon them from the mouth of the canyon.

Another family had been engaged in research. The father, who is an archaeologist, had come back from Cairo with some priceless treasures that had been excavated. All of them were destroyed in a moment.

Another family had stuffed some of their belongings into a station wagon as rapidly as they could, leaving just enough room for the children. They all piled in, but couldn't find their keys. So they got out and ran for their lives. When they returned, everything had melted right down to the cement slab . . . even parts of the car.

One man who realized the fire was coming soon made a list of the things he didn't want to forget. But the fire came so fast that the only thing he saved was the list!

The psalmist says that even if the earth should change, mountains should quake, and fire should roar, God is our bridge over troubled waters.

But is He really? Is God that relevant? We need to search

ourselves with complete honesty to see where God fits—both now and when trouble strikes.

Look what the Scriptures promise:

Do not fear, for I am with you;
Do not anxiously look about you, for I am your God.
(Is. 41:10)

For God has not given us a spirit of timidity, but of power and love and discipline. (2 Tim. 1:7)

Be strong and courageous! (Josh. 1:9)

The LORD is my light and my salvation;
Whom shall I fear?
The LORD is the defense of my life;
Whom shall I dread? (Ps. 27:1)

For my father and my mother have forsaken me,
But the LORD will take me up. (Ps. 27:10)

In extreme assaults of stress, God invites us to rest in His eternal embrace.

Standing Fast

Next, we move to a section of Psalm 46 that talks about the city you live in. Nations and kingdoms are rising up against the city. But verse 5 says: "God is in the midst of her, she will not be moved." The word *moved* comes from the Hebrew term that means "to totter or to shake."

The phrase "all shook up" was made popular by the late Elvis Presley. Born dirt poor in a little town in Mississippi, he was an only child. He had little encouragement and no special skills. At the age of eighteen, making fourteen dollars a week as a truck driver, he decided to make a recording, just on a lark. You know the rest of the story. He became the best-paid male entertainer in the history of America.

But Elvis Presley said shortly before his death that he would pay a million dollars for one week of a normal life of peace, to be able to move up and down the streets of his city without harassment.

I heard Pat Boone interviewed shortly after Elvis's untimely death. He said, "I cared a lot for Elvis. But he went in the wrong direction. Ironically, we met for the last time when I was going to do a show back east and he was going to Vegas. He said to me, 'Say, Pat, where are you going?' I told him where I was going and how I looked forward to being involved in some kind of Christian ministry. He said, 'Hey, I'm going to Vegas. Pat, as long as I've known you, you've been going in the wrong direction.' I answered, 'Elvis, that just depends on where you're coming from.'" America's highest-paid male entertainer was the personification of stress.

Elvis found that money won't alleviate stress. This forty-two-year-old man—whose funeral brought over five tons of flowers from people who drove night after night or took international flights to get to Memphis—this man, who would have given a million dollars for a week of peace, lived his life all shook up. That very theme became his personal trademark.

The psalmist said, "When the city is under siege and under threat, I will not be moved. I will not shake, because the God of hope is with us."

He is also in us.

Ceasing to Strive

Look at the third part of Psalm 46 (v. 10), describing the plaguing depression that often accompanies the aftermath of death. God says, "Cease striving and know that I am God." The word *striving* has been added by the translators; I believe it is acceptable because it explains the meaning with consistency. But perhaps it takes away a bit of the impact of the single word cease. The Hebrew term, used here, *raphah,* means "relax"! The point is that you will never discover the tent of power God can build over you if you keep racing. Stress will ultimately win out.

> Slow me down, Lord.
>
> Ease the pounding of my heart by the quieting of my mind.
>
> Steady my hurried pace with a vision of the eternal reach of time.
>
> Give me, amid the confusion of the day, the calmness of the everlasting hills.
>
> Break the tensions of my nerves and muscles with the soothing music of the singing streams that live in my memory.
>
> Teach me the art of taking minute vacations—
>
>> of slowing down to look at a flower,
>>
>> to chat with a friend,
>>
>> to pat a dog, to smile at a child,
>>
>> to read a few lines from a good book.
>
> Slow me down, Lord, and inspire me to send my roots deep into the soil of life's enduring values, that I may grow toward my greater destiny.
>
> Remind me each day that the race is not always to the swift; that there is more to life than increasing its speed.

Let me look upward to the towering oak and know that
it grew great and strong because it grew slowly and well.[4]

In order for the Lord God to counteract the incredible toll
that stress takes on us, we *must* slow down.

Stop and think. When was the last time you sat around the
table after supper just to relax and have a little fun? When was
the last time you flew a kite, took a long walk in the woods,
pedaled a bike in the local park, drove *under* the speed limit,
made something with your own hands, kicked back and drank
in an hour of good music, or strolled along the surf at sunset?
When was the last time you took off your watch for an entire
Saturday, or carried a little kid on your shoulders, or read a
chapter in a tub of warm water, or enjoyed life so deeply you
couldn't quit smiling? Small wonder you're under stress!

I'll never forget the testimony of an anonymous friar in a
Nebraska monastery. He wrote it in a letter late in his life. It's
not what we would expect in a "religious testimony" . . . maybe
that's why I appreciate it so much!

If I had my life to live over again, I'd try to make more
mistakes next time.

I would relax, I would limber up, I would be sillier than
I have been this trip.

I know of very few things I would take seriously. I would
take more trips. I would be crazier. I would climb more
mountains, swim more rivers, and watch more sunsets.

I would do more walking and looking.

I would eat more ice cream and less beans.

I would have more actual troubles, and fewer imaginary
ones.

You see, I'm one of those people who lives life prophy-lactically and sensibly hour after hour, day after day. Oh, I've had my moments, and if I had to do it over again I'd have more of them.

In fact, I'd try to have nothing else, just moments, one after another, instead of living so many years ahead each day. I've been one of those people who never goes anywhere without a thermometer, a hot-water bottle, a gargle, a rain-coat, aspirin, and a parachute.

If I had to do it over again I would go places, do things, and travel lighter than I have.

If I had my life to live over I would start barefooted ear-lier in the spring and stay that way later in the fall.

I would play hookey more. I wouldn't make such good grades, except by accident. I would ride on more merry-go-rounds. I'd pick more daisies.[5]

It is fairly safe to say that this old gentleman had his fill of stress. He realized that to break its spell one must break the mold of a rat-race lifestyle. May his tribe increase!

My Stress—God's Strength

Let me leave with you three very practical thoughts regarding this matter of God's strength through stress, as found in Psalm 46.

First, His strength is immediately available. Our trials are *not* superficial or irrelevant. They are vehicles of grace that God uses to bring us growth. I read in one of Stuart Briscoe's books of a man who went to his physician, complaining of constant headaches. The physician asked him if he smoked.

"Yes, I do," said the fellow.

"Well, stop smoking," suggested the physician.

So he stopped, but the headaches persisted. He went back.

"Do you drink?"

"Yeah, I drink considerably."

"Stop it."

So he stopped. The headaches persisted.

"Are you engaged in physical labor that would in some way put pressure on your back?"

"Yes I am."

"Quit your job."

He quit his job and took another position, but his headaches persisted. Every day the pain pulsed through his head.

Finally, they discovered he was wearing a size 15 collar on a size 16 neck. No wonder he had a headache![6]

Superficial problems call for superficial solutions. But real life isn't like that; its headaches and stresses go deeper, right down to the bone. They touch the nerve areas of our security. But God says He is a present help in trouble. He is immediately available. Do you realize that wherever you travel, whatever the time of day, you can call and He will answer? He never even asks you to make an appointment. He never puts you on hold. No, He says, "I'll help you right now." He's a very present and immediate help.

The second thing I observe about God's power in this psalm is that it is overpowering! It's a tent that can stretch over *any* stress—in fact, it's tailor-made for stress. Nothing is bigger than the power of God. Isn't that beautiful!

Furthermore, His power is not dependent on our help. You're weak, remember? Have you felt that weakness lately?

Probably. Are your life-change units reaching 300 or more? If so, God is ready to assist.

The winter of 1966 brought a terrible blizzard to New England. We lived there at that time and had just our two older children. Cynthia, the kids, and I had gone to a special performance one afternoon. We were novices concerning blizzards, not believing that the storm report was anything to worry about. We drove down to the Boston Garden and parked our car a number of blocks away.

The Ice Follies was a beautiful display of artistic skating. We thoroughly enjoyed the show.

When we bundled up and stepped outside, we came to the stark realization that we should have believed the weather report. The snow stood about four feet deep!

I remember picking up our older child, Curt; Cynthia carried Charissa, and we were both on our way. We trudged through the snow and could feel the hot breath of the children against our ears. All along the way, we kept reassuring them that it would be all right, that we were going to make it.

As we neared the car, we weren't sure which one it was because there were mounds of snow packed on top of each car. Snow began to accumulate on our coats, and we shook it off as best we could. I was looking at car after car. Panic began to seize me. Finally, we got to our car, dug it out, and hurriedly scraped the ice off the windshield.

I tried to push the key into the door keyhole. It was frozen solid. By then, all of us were shivering. I banged my fist against the keyhole time after time. The wind cut through our heavy coats.

Finally, we got the door open and the kids tucked in the backseat. One of them looked at us and said, "We love you,

Daddy and Momma. Thanks." That's all I needed. I felt like a million dollars when I heard that. Just, "Daddy, I love you." As we drove off, those words warmed me within.

That's all our Father asks. You can't carry yourself through the storms; it's too much for you. When will we come to the realization that the blizzards in our lives are allowed by God? Those threatening storms are designed to slow us down, to make us climb up into His arms, to force us to depend on Him.

Maybe it's time to say, "Lord, I love You. Thank You. Through Your strength, I will not be moved. I will stop running, stop striving. I will not fear. I will hold on to You. I will count on You to build that tent around me and protect me from the blast. Thank You for giving me, in love, this blizzard of stress. Thank You that I can't even see the distance or the goal. I admit my weakness. I need Your strength."

4

As I wrote these words, an enormous fire was raging across a canyon about thirty miles north of my home. I had just turned off a televised newscast in which a couple was interviewed. They stood arm in arm, stunned. Their quarter-of-a-million-dollar home had just gone up in smoke. They had spent eleven years saving for and building their "dream." In less than thirty minutes, it was reduced to a pile of smoldering ashes.

Several states in the Southeast—Louisiana, Mississippi, and Alabama—had been ravaged by devastating hurricanes. Floods, vicious winds, and looters had taken their toll. The loss amounted to millions of dollars, perhaps half a billion in all.

Just before coming home that evening, I spent about an hour with a woman whose husband had died.

Also, a member of our church had to be admitted to a local hospital that afternoon. He might lose his arm to cancer.

It's easy to miss the things God has to teach us because we cannot imagine Him being involved in the grief or disappointment or heartache brought on by the loss of someone or something dear to us. But some of His choicest deliveries come through the back doors of our lives. These unanticipated setbacks are sprung on us, and often we're not ready to take them on in the particular package in which God delivers them. Therefore, it's easy to miss them.

Losses come in two categories, generally speaking.

The Loss of Those You Love

Joe Bayly most unexpectedly lost three of his children to death, two of them while they were teenagers. He later wrote a book, *The View from a Hearse,* in which he talked about losing significant people.[1] It was a blow!

When my good friend Joyce Landorf endured the pain of losing her precious mother, she shared the depth of her sorrow with all of us in *Mourning Song*—one of her best books.[2]

But maybe you don't have the gift of expressing your loss so eloquently. The person you have lost might be a relative or close friend or working partner, and you are experiencing that loss alone. You have lost that person either by death or by distance—either way, you've lost him. You've enjoyed his fellowship and companionship, and suddenly by death or by his moving away, you no longer have him near. The person is no longer visibly present.

That is one kind of loss that's hard to bear. Have you ever considered God's message in the loss of those you love?

The Loss of Things You Love

The second category is the loss of personal necessities or benefits—the loss of a job, the loss of a desire or a goal or a dream in life (and we all have such dreams, or should have—what would life be without dreams?). The loss occurs and, suddenly, you know you will never realize the dream you've had in your heart.

Job: A Man Who Lost It All

In this chapter, we will look at the painfully familiar story of

Job. He lost both people and things. It is easy to glamorize and immortalize this man who is known for his patience according to James, "the patience of Job." But I want you to feel with him the awful blow of his losses.

Bear in mind that the Bible is a book of *reality*. That's the one thing that attracted me to it years ago. It doesn't glamorize the saints; it tells the truth about them. It paints them as they are. When they act as men of God, it reveals them as such. And when they fail, it discloses that. It doesn't hedge.

Look at the list of Job's spiritual and material possessions. First of all, he had godliness. The Scripture says he was "blameless, upright, fearing God, and turning away from evil" (Job 1:1). You can't get much better than that! He was an incredible man of God, a man who was greatly respected.

Second, he had a large family. Seven sons and three daughters were born to him—ten children in all. That's quite a "quiver" full (see Ps. 127:3–5).

Third, he had abundant possessions, including seven thousand sheep, three thousand camels, five hundred yoke of oxen, five hundred female donkeys, and servants by the dozens.

Fourth, he had prestige. The Hebrew text literally says Job was the "heaviest" of all the men of the East. That doesn't mean fat; it's an ancient expression meaning prosperous. He was notoriously popular. People knew about Job. Most biblical scholars believe that Job lived in the days of the patriarchs, that he was a contemporary of Abraham. His name was a household word.

I want it to be understood that, humanly speaking, Job did not deserve the losses he suffered. *All losses do not come because of wrong.* Some of God's people who suffer greatly don't deserve it from a human point of view. It especially is to those people I want to speak.

The fact is, Job was godly. He had a good family and he took excellent care of them. He continued praying for his children even after they were grown. They had their own homes, so we know he was moving on in years. The biblical text says nothing about his health, his age, or his business. It simply describes a very comfortable, prosperous, secure man of God.

Some might think as they read those words, "Well, who wouldn't walk with God in a lifestyle like that? I mean, with such a security hedge around him, who wouldn't stand with the Lord?"

That's exactly the approach Satan used before the Lord: "You have a hedge built around him. If You touch him, he'll curse You."

Here's how the story went. Try your best to picture the scene; don't skip a line.

Now it happened on the day when his sons and his daughters were eating and drinking wine in their oldest brother's house, that a messenger came to Job and said, "The oxen were plowing and the donkeys feeding beside them, and the Sabeans attacked and took them. They also slew the servants with the edge of the sword, and I alone have escaped to tell you."

While he was still speaking, another also came and said, "The fire of God fell from heaven and burned up the sheep and the servants and consumed them, and I alone have escaped to tell you."

While he was still speaking, another also came and said, "The Chaldeans formed three bands and made a raid on the camels and took them and slew the servants with the edge of the sword; and I alone have escaped to tell you."

While he was still speaking, another also came and said, "Your sons and your daughters were eating and drinking wine in their oldest brother's house, and behold, a great wind came from across the wilderness and struck the four corners of the house, and it fell on the young people and they died; and I alone have escaped to tell you." (Job 1:13–19, italics mine)

Just like that! Did you sense the rapid, blow-by-blow movement of the account? Here was Job secure, comfortable, and safe. Then having just brought his sons and daughters before God in prayer, they died one after another, without warning. He lost all ten adult children.

How did he respond? He started out by saying, "Naked. . ." Isn't that interesting? Open-handed, dependent, having nothing in himself, head shaved, robe torn—Job is the picture of utter dependence. He worships the Lord and says, "Naked I came from my mother's womb, and naked I shall return there. The Lord gave and the Lord has taken away. Blessed be the name of the Lord" (Job 1:21).

He didn't fling his fists toward heaven and swear at God. He prayed. Neither did he submerge himself in self-pity and groan, "Why me?" No, he worshiped.

It is tempting to think, "Well, he was some kind of guy, some kind of Six-Million-Dollar Christian. I'm not cut out like that; it's not my world."

But Job was not all that special. He was simply a man of God. His lifestyle was linked with God's so beautifully that he didn't get sidetracked.

Did he grieve? The balance of the book will tell you that he did.

Was he a realist? In every sense of the word. But he didn't blame God; he didn't sin. That tells me *it can be done.* That tells me, moms and dads, that through God's power you can pull off a vital trust in Christ when calamity strikes. Businessmen, students: When you see your dream die and you think that's the end, when you see that romance go over the edge, God says, "Hey, I'm still here. Remember Me?" Such times season us. They temper us . . . mature us. Losses put steel into our otherwise fragile lives.

A member of our pastoral staff made a very insightful comment to me recently. He said, "Part of the difficulty with the person I've been counseling is that he's *never really suffered a severe loss. He's almost spoiled with life.*" That can happen easily.

So our friend Job didn't blame God and didn't sin. Looking for a logical reason, we think, "Well, at least he had his health." Turn the page.

> Then Satan went out from the presence of the LORD, and smote Job with sore boils from the sole of his foot to the crown of his head. And he took a potsherd to scrape himself while he was sitting among the ashes. (Job 2:7–8)

How awful!

One authority on disease says this condition resembles the plague mentioned in Deuteronomy 28:27, 35. Here is an idea of what Job endured.

> The LORD will smite you with the boils of Egypt and

with tumors and with the scab and with the itch, from which you cannot be healed. (v. 27)

The LORD will strike you on the knees and legs with sore boils, from which you cannot be healed, from the sole of your foot to the crown of your head. (v. 35)

Dr. Meredith Kline, an Old Testament scholar, offers this vivid description of Job's illness:

Modern medical opinion is not unanimous in its diagnosis of Job's disease, but according to the prognosis in Job's day, it was apparently hopeless. The horrible symptoms included inflamed eruptions accompanied by intense itching (2:7–8), maggots in ulcers (7:5), erosion of the bones (30:17), blackening and falling off of skin (30:30), and terrifying nightmares (7:14), though some of these may possibly be attributed to the prolonged exposure that followed the onset of the disease. Job's whole body, it seems, was rapidly smitten with the loathsome, painful symptoms.[3]

What a tragic picture! Job is covered from the top of his head to the bottom of his feet with those oozing, itching ulcers, and he's sitting there in the ashes scratching them with pieces of pottery. When you have experienced a loss, have you ever wondered why God leaves some things behind and takes others? Sometimes what he leaves seems strange to you. I have in mind Job's wife! She said to him: "Do you still hold fast your integrity? Curse God and die!" (Job 2:9)

Who on earth needs advice like that? Bayly mentions in his book that one of the best contributions we can make to a person going through intense suffering and loss is our presence *without* words, not even verses of Scripture dumped into the ears of the grieving. He said:

> Don't try to "prove" anything to a survivor. An arm about the shoulder, a firm grip of the hand, a kiss: these are the proofs grief needs, not logical reasoning.
>
> I was sitting, torn by grief. Someone came and talked to me of God's dealings, of why it happened, of hope beyond the grave. He talked constantly, he said things I knew were true.
>
> I was unmoved, except to wish he'd go away. He finally did.
>
> Another came and sat beside me. He didn't talk. He didn't ask leading questions. He just sat beside me for an hour or more, listened when I said something, answered briefly, prayed simply, left.
>
> I was moved. I was comforted. I hated to see him go.[4]

An individual reeling from the blow of calamity has a broken heart. The soil of his soul is not ready for the implanting of the heavenly seed. He will be later, but not right away. Nor is he ready for some extreme word of counsel like, "Curse God and die!"

(Mrs. Job, incidentally, is mentioned only one other time in the whole Bible. Her great contribution to Job's life would be her counsel here in 2:9 and later in 19:17. There Job comments, "My breath is offensive to my wife." Can you believe it?)

My phone rang one Monday morning. A good friend of mine in our church tried hard to speak, but his voice broke. He wanted to meet with me—as soon as possible. He told me my counsel was absolutely vital. He apologized for interrupting me on my day off, but it couldn't wait.

Of course, I dropped everything. We met in my study less than thirty minutes later. He stumbled in, weeping audibly as we embraced. I sensed immediately that Clifford (not his real name) was in no condition for a lot of high-powered advice or even a reminder of what I had preached only twenty-four hours ago.

Between sobs and lengthy pauses of total silence (so important in the counseling process), I said virtually nothing. Cliff's wife had just returned from seeing her physician. After extensive testing and a thorough battery of diagnostic exams, it was certain she had a malignancy of the lymph glands—and it was the kind that had a very bleak prognosis, even if she endured the miserable chemotherapy treatments. It was, understandably, devastating news.

For almost an hour he poured out his anguish, his fears, his confusion. The man was knowledgeable in the Scripture. He and his wife faithfully attended Sunday services. They both loved Christ. But that was no time for him to be told a lot of stuff . . . even true stuff. He needed a listening ear, plain and simple.

Funny thing, as Cliff left he embraced me again and thanked me for my counsel. I really don't believe I said ten sentences the entire time.

When you have friends who are going through valleys, they will appreciate so very much just the fact that you care. Your presence, some gracious act, a warm embrace—these kinds of things best show your love. In fact, just sitting beside them and crying with them often helps the most.

God's Great Goal

I want you to read what is, in my opinion, one of the most profound verses in the Bible.

> But he said to her, "You speak as one of the foolish women speaks. [Now here it is, so please mark it with pencil or in your mind. Etch it there and call on it when calamity strikes.] Shall we indeed accept good from God and not accept adversity?" In all this Job did not sin with his lips. (Job 2:10)

Amen! Job's God was not some gracious creature who sat on the edge of heaven, dropping good little gifts wrapped in silver out of the sky, saying, "That will make you happy. That'll please you." That's not the God of heaven. The sovereign God of heaven disposes and dispenses what brings glory to Himself. *He brings to us not only good, but adversity as well.* Our great God isn't obligated to make us comfortable.

Did you see that truth? "Shall we indeed accept good (oh, we're quick to do that) and not adversity?" Are you *ready* to accept adversity? In the flesh, in the horizontal perspective, you'll resent it; you'll run from it; you'll build up a bitterness against Him, saying, "What kind of a God is that?" But in the spiritual dimension, you will recognize that He had a *right* to bring the unpleasant as well as the pleasant. Without this concept, you'll never be able to persevere through pressure. It will blow you away!

Listen, our major goal in life is *not* to be happy or satisfied, but to glorify God. That cuts across the grain of our Western culture. Every father's goal for his family is that they be happy and satisfied. Very few—precious few—fathers have as their family's goal that the family glorify God first. We work our fingers to the bone to the last day of our lives so that we might be happy and satisfied—and all we have to show for it is bony fingers. No, God's great goal for our lives is to glorify Him, as the apostle Paul said, "Whether by life or by death" (Phil. 1:20).

Listen to Job's counsel when the calamities die down:

> Behold, how happy is the man whom God reproves,
> So do not despise the discipline of the Almighty.
> For He inflicts pain, and gives relief;
> He wounds, and His hands also heal.
> From six troubles He will deliver you,
> Even in seven evil will not touch you.
> In famine He will redeem you from death,
> And in war from the power of the sword.
> You will be hidden from the scourge of the tongue,
> Neither will you be afraid of violence when it comes.
> You will laugh at violence and famine. (Job 5:17–22)

You see, God's great goal for us is not that we be comfortable or satisfied, nor that we live out a "wonderful plan" of constant smiling, being happy, facing no calamity, no evil, and no difficulty. It is *wrong* to tell the non-Christian, "Trust God and your worries are over. . . . Believe in Jesus and you'll never know what it is to be defeated again." That's unfair. It is downright unbiblical!

Instead, why not be honest and say, "Believe in Jesus Christ, and you might step into a world of testing you never knew before, because you will have become the object of Jesus Himself, and His character traits are to be formed in your life.

And frankly, you can't have them formed without the fire and the loss. Since our goal is to glorify Christ, we can expect some loss." That's accurate!

When you suffer and lose, that does not mean you are being disobedient. In fact, it might mean you're right in the center of His will. The path of obedience is often marked by times of suffering and loss.

Job honestly admits, "'Behold, I go forward but He is not there'" (Job 23:8). Now here's a man with a rotting, decaying body; no children; and a nagging wife. He is heavy of heart and goes out at night looking for God. He cries out: "I look, and He's not there!" Losses are lonely times of crisis.

> And backward, but I cannot perceive Him;
> When He acts on the left, I cannot behold Him;
> He turns on the right, I cannot see Him. (Job 23:8–9)

When you've been through times like this, you know *exactly* what Job is saying.

The Right Perspective

Christian, remember that God knows the way.

> But He knows the way I take;
> When He has tried me, I shall come forth as gold [implying that there will be an end to it].
> My foot has held fast to His path;
> I have kept His way and not turned aside.
> I have not departed from the command of His lips;

I have treasured the words of His mouth more than my
    necessary food.
But He is unique and who can turn Him?
And what His soul desires, that He does.
For He performs what is appointed for me,
And many such decrees are with Him. (Job 23:10–14)

How marvelous! This is the hardest thing in the world to
claim. When I've lost it all and I turn to a verse like that and it
says, "He's appointed it for me," do you know what I have to do?
I have to change *my* perspective. I have to force myself to see it
from His point of view. What is often considered a loss *now*
leads to a gain *later*. The Lord restored Job's fortunes, and He
increased all that he had—twofold. He *doubled* his prosperity!

Now be careful not to make this specific situation into a
general principle. It's easy for us to think, "Okay, I had a
$33,000-a-year job. Now that I've lost it, God's going to give
me a $60,000-a-year job next month. Everything is going to be
great! My checkbook will always balance . . . my car won't ever
break down." That kind of thinking reduces Almighty God to
Santa Claus and the Tooth Fairy and Aladdin's Lamp all
wrapped up into one. Our Lord's blessings aren't always tan-
gible or measurable in dollars and cents.

When He rewards after loss, He builds internal character
traits. He gives a deep peace. He provides things money cannot
touch. Security replaces insecurity. We receive purpose and
renewed direction. We gain an understanding, compassionate
heart—along with wisdom we never had before.

Isn't it interesting how you can be all involved in your own
little world, your own little house, and then one day you take
an airplane flight, and it changes your perspective? The plane

climbs to 15,000 . . . 25,000 . . . 30,000 feet—and what do you see? You see a whole world down there! Your perspective is altered, because you are no longer looking at life from the viewpoint of one little room, nor are you worried about the color of one little drape.

That's where He dwells. He puts it all together like a beautiful piece of tapestry. Every once in a while, you get a glimpse of the underside, and you see the knots and the crummy part of it and you think, "What in the world is wrong?" His whole view is from the other side; He sees everything at once.

Have you recently suffered a loss? Maybe the wound is still tender; maybe it's too early to know why. Frankly, you may *never* know why! But through it all, believe me, God has not left you. He is there. He will never walk away.

Margaret Powers once told of a man whose life was marked by hardship. He was a Christian, but life was not easy. One loss followed another, and disappointment and pain seemed to be his closest friends.

One night he had a dream. He was with the Lord, looking back on his life, which was portrayed as footprints along a sandy beach. Usually there were two sets of footprints—his and the Savior's. But as he looked closer, he saw only one set of footprints along the very rugged places. He frowned, confused, and asked the Lord:

"Look there. You and I have walked together during much of my lifetime . . . but when things got really bad, where'd You go? I needed You at those times more than ever. Why'd You leave?"

The answer came: "My child, I have never left you. The two sets of footprints assure you of that. But there were times when it was almost more than you could bear. At those very, very hard times, I carried you in My arms. The single set of foot-prints you see at those perilous places are Mine. That was when I was carrying you."

We may feel alone, forsaken, and forgotten, but we are not. In time of loss, our God picks us up and holds us close.

5

Impossibilities: Uncrossable Rivers of Life

We often find ourselves bogging down in our spiritual growth simply because the challenges before us look absolutely impossible. Such frustrations are not new. The one who composed this little chorus must have experienced those feelings too.

> Got any rivers you think are uncrossable;
> Got any mountains you can't tunnel through?
> God specializes in things tho't impossible;
> He does the things others cannot do.[1]

If you are not currently in such a bind, it will not be long until you will be. If things seem a little difficult today, just wait: they'll soon be impossible! Uncrossable rivers, untunneled mountains, and impossible circumstances really aren't unusual. How do you handle them? Where do you get the faith to meet them?

"Impossible" Scriptures

To put everything into the right perspective, I would like us to begin by looking at four key passages of Scripture that address the subject of impossibilities. Two of them are in Jeremiah 32 and two are in the Gospel of Luke. The prophet Jeremiah wrote:

Ah Lord GOD! Behold, Thou hast made the heavens and the earth by Thy great power and by Thine outstretched arm! Nothing is too difficult for Thee. (Jer. 32:17)

Read that sentence again: "Nothing is too difficult for Thee." Do you realize that whatever thing or things you're calling "impossibilities" could be superimposed over what God says is "nothing" to Him? *Nothing!*

It's difficult to reconstruct in the English language the full color and impact of the Hebrew words used in this verse. The best we can do is to say: "No, absolutely nothing for You is extraordinary or surpassing." The text begins with the strongest negative known to the Hebrew language. "No, nothing, absolutely nothing for You, Lord, is extraordinary." What a statement to ponder!

Jeremiah 32:27 is the second verse I want you to see.

Behold, I am the LORD, the God of all flesh; is anything too difficult for me?

Look at the last part of that verse a second time: "Is anything too difficult for me?" God is asking you to substitute your impossibilities for the word "anything." You fill in the blank. "Is _____ too difficult for Me?" The implied answer, of course, is: "Absolutely not. Nothing is too difficult for Me."

You may be sitting there thinking, "Yeah, that may be true for Christians who have a lot of past miracles in their repertoires. But you don't know my situation."

I don't have to know your situation. All I need to know—and all you need to know—is God and His promises. He is Lord, the bottom line of life, and nothing is too difficult for *Him*.

Next, look at Luke 1:37. I want you to connect those passages in Jeremiah with this message in Luke. It is an answer to Mary's question concerning her conception. An angel appeared to her and said "You are going to bear the Christ-child."

She asks, "How can this be, since I am a virgin? How is that possible?"

Do you recall the answer given to her? It's what we just read in Jeremiah—"For nothing will be impossible with God." To make that statement practical, the word "nothing" can be replaced with your situation. Whatever it is, it is not impossible with God.

In Luke 18:27, Jesus Christ said, "'The things impossible with men are possible with God.'"

Close your eyes for a moment. I want you to think about that which seems most impossible. You have seen and read these four promises of God. Each has said virtually the same thing: Nothing is impossible with God. That includes your river, your mountain, any impossibility. Is it your business? Or your school? Or your marriage? How about keeping the house clean, keeping up with the wash, having a ministry with others, or healing strained relationships with people? Will you ask the Lord to handle that specific impossibility, and then leave it with Him in a faith that simply will not doubt?

DO

    THAT

        RIGHT

            NOW . . .

                PLEASE!

One "Impossible" Event

In John 6 we find not only a familiar event, but a unique one, for several reasons.

First, it is the only miracle mentioned in all four Gospels, so it seems to be extremely significant to the Gospel writers, and certainly to the Lord Himself.

Second, it is the only account in which Jesus asked the advice of someone else.

Third, it is the only time Jesus performed a miracle before such a huge crowd.

Fourth, it is an "absolute" miracle. That is, it is not some natural thing that was altered slightly on a sliding scale. In fact, I have chosen this miracle because it seems so impossible.

John 6 begins with three words that are of importance to the setting: "After these things. . ." When you read these words in your Bible, always ask yourself, "What things?" John's account of this miracle is preceded by five other chapters, and if you suddenly come into the midst of the story it is like beginning a novel in the middle. So we need to ask "After *what* things?"

Jesus has chosen His disciples and sent them out for ministry. According to Matthew, they have gone to every village in the area and proclaimed the gospel of the kingdom, the message of repentance. Now they are back with Jesus, tired and weary. They've preached in every nook and cranny. They are physically exhausted, emotionally worn, and the Lord desires to be alone with them and to rest. (It is important for all of us in our work—and the Lord Jesus is an illustration of this—to have times of refreshment.) He wanted to provide His hardworking men the opportunity to get away from the crowd.

> After these things Jesus went away to the other side of the sea of Galilee (or Tiberias). And a great multitude was following Him. . . . And Jesus went up on the mountain, and there He sat with His disciples. (John 6:1–3)

Picture the scene. Jesus and His twelve are alone on the mountain. They are there for some "R and R." Then, in John 6:5, we read:

> Jesus therefore lifting up His eyes, and seeing that a great multitude was coming to him. . .

They are tired and weary, and they want to be alone. Jesus looked up and saw an enormous crowd approaching. According to verse 10, the number was about five thousand. Matthew 14:21 tells us it was five thousand *plus* the women and children. So it would be safe to say there could have been eight to ten thousand people coming up that mountain. That's a lot of folks—and a lot of needs!

Here they are in a barren place, and wouldn't you know, the tribe is hungry. And no grocery store! The disciples don't know anyone, and they aren't aware of any source of food. It's an *impossible* situation.

But *that's how Jesus wanted it,* because those disciples are just like you and me. "Oh no, Lord. What on earth can we do?" That's the way we disciples look at it, but Jesus saw it as a perfect opportunity for a Class A miracle. He had explained to them that He was God's Son, God in the flesh. They had learned that theory back in their boot-camp days. Now was their chance to see Him in action. It was time for sterile theory to be replaced with solid reality.

So He gave them a test. The first one to take the exam was Philip. He is mentioned by name in verse 5.

> Jesus therefore lifting up His eyes, and seeing that a great multitude was coming to Him, said to Philip, "Where are we to buy bread, that these may eat?"

Philip was probably not the smartest one in the group. (I personally believe Judas was the sharpest of the Twelve. That is often true of wolves and false prophets, by the way.) And Philip was not the one in charge of supplies. Judas was treasurer, but he didn't ask Judas. Why not?

Before we answer that, let's look at the next verse. It takes all the pressure off.

> And this He was saying to test him; for He Himself knew what He was intending to do.

Jesus knew what He was intending to do. He always does! The learning process is for *our* benefit. He knows how we're going to wind up, but He doesn't put us in some cosmic time machine and catapult us to the end. He lets us grind through the experience. Remember, He wants us to persevere *through* the pressure, trusting Him during impossible situations.

So He said to Philip, "Where are we going to find bread to feed them?" Why Philip? To test him. He wanted to ascertain the depth of his faith. He wanted to determine, "Has Philip learned how to trust Me? Will Philip focus on My ability while standing neck deep in *his* impossibility?"

I want to give you just a little insight into Philip. It makes you appreciate even more that Jesus asked *him*. Philip was the one who later said to the Lord, "Just let us see God and we won't have any more questions." Philip was the fellow who had to *see* everything. He was what I call a "statistical pessimist." He had a slide rule for a mind, and if he could figure it all out—great.

How easy it is to dress up doubt in neat-sounding, logical, sophisticated garb! Philip never even answered Jesus' question. Instead, he replied: "Two hundred denarii worth of bread is not sufficient for them, for every one to receive a little."

That's not the question! The Lord had asked, "Where are we going to go to get bread to feed these eight to ten thousand people?" And Philip said, "Two hundred denarii worth of bread will not feed them." That's two different conversations: the Lord asked him, "Where do we go?" and Philip's answer dealt with "how much."

A denarius, by the way, was worth about seventeen cents. It equaled a man's daily wage. (How about that, you who think you have it rough.) Seventeen cents times two hundred is thirty-four dollars in our terms. Thirty-four dollars wouldn't give each person a crumb and a cup of tea.

The statistical pessimist! All the Lord wanted Philip to say was, "I don't know. It's impossible with *me*, but it's nothing to you and I'm going to wait and see what You're going to do. You are a Specialist, Lord, in situations like this." But that's not what Philip said.

The testing was not over. Another fellow, who is of still more interesting significance to us, came on the scene. His name was Andrew. He was as different from Philip as night and day. Philip saw only the *situation*, the size of the problem. He did not remember how big God is. He was more convinced of what could *not* be done than what could be done.

If you are a Philip, that's the way you are. When someone

61

suggests a new idea, you say, "Oh, no. That won't work." Or when some situation gets worse and you cannot handle it any longer, it never dawns on you to simply trust God. All you can see is what can't be done. There are a lot of people like that in God's family.

I once heard about a farmer who was continually optimistic, seldom discouraged or blue. He had a neighbor who was just the opposite. Grim and gloomy, he faced each new morning with a heavy sigh.

The happy, optimistic farmer would see the sun coming up and shout over the roar of the tractor, "Look at that beautiful sun and the clear sky!" And with a frown, the negative neighbor would reply, "Yeah—it'll probably scorch the crops!"

When clouds would gather and much-needed rain would start to fall, our positive friend would smile across the fence, "Ain't this great—God is giving our corn a drink today!" Again, the same negative response, "Uh huh . . . but if it doesn't stop 'fore long it'll flood and wash everything away."

One day the optimist decided to put his pessimistic neighbor to the maximum test. He bought the smartest, most expensive bird dog he could find. He trained him to do things no other dog on earth could do—impossible feats that would surely astound anyone.

He invited the pessimist to go duck hunting with him. They sat in the boat, hidden in the duck blind. In came the ducks. Both men fired and several ducks fell into the water. "Go get 'em!" ordered the owner with a gleam in his eye. The dog leaped out of the boat, walked *on* the water, and picked up the birds one by one.

"Well, what do ya think of that?"

Unsmiling, the pessimist answered, "He can't swim, can he?" Philip was that kind of guy, pessimistic to the core.

John 6:8 says: "One of His disciples, Andrew, Simon Peter's brother, said to Him. . ." (I feel a little sorry for Andrew. Every time he is mentioned, he is called Simon Peter's brother. Ever thought about that?)

Andrew had one strong thing going for him, however. Any man who can talk a little fella out of his lunch must have some degree of persuasion! He said, "There is a lad here who has five barley loaves and two fish." How did he know that? Well, he must have been inside his lunch sack, that's how he knew. He had probably been rustling through the crowd, seeing who had what. He approached the Lord and said, "Here's five loaves and two fish."

But he didn't stop there. He went on, "But what are these for so many people?" Too bad he didn't stop when he was ahead. He volunteered information he wasn't even asked. It is almost as though he put the lunch sack down and walked away with a shrug. The Lord didn't even answer him. Such "little thinking" turned Him off!

This is applicable for all of us "Andrews" who are hard-working and diligent, but who are shot down by the prospect of the odds being against us.

You hear of the needs of the unreached multitudes. A whole world out there is aching to know Christ. You tuck the little ones in bed at night—two, three, four children. "Lord, they are yours, but what are these among so many?"

You don't have a whole lot of money, so you are able to give just $45 month after month. You begin to calculate, "What's this among so many needs?"

You don't have a lot of time. Your work takes up ten or twelve hours a day, and you think, "I often don't have but five or ten minutes for prayer. That hardly counts."

The woman who composed the hymn "O Zion, Haste" must have had the Andrews in mind when she wrote:

Give of thy sons to bear the message glorious,
Give of thy wealth to speed them on their way;
Pour out thy soul for them in prayer victorious,
And all thou spendest, Jesus will repay.[2]

Maybe you don't have a lot to give, but that's all that little fellow had, and that's all Andrew could find, and that's all the Lord needed. *Just that.*

Now, the miracle. Remember the story? It's as simple a miracle as it can be. In quiet, unobtrusive fashion, Jesus said to the disciples, "Have the people sit down" (John 6:10). You see, the Twelve are going to be personally involved in carrying out the miracle, because the miracle was basically for *their* benefit, not the multitude's. He could have fed the thousands anything they wanted any time of the day, but He used the disciples as ushers.

The people sat down as they were told. Then Scripture says:

Jesus therefore took the loaves; and having given thanks, He distributed to those who were seated; likewise also of the fish as much as they wanted. (John 6:11)

You can't fully appreciate this unless you understand that the word *fish* was the word used for little pickled fish, like a sardine, not a great big sea bass or salmon. And barley loaves were the size of large pancakes—flat, hard, and brittle—the bread of poor people.

Jesus took these brittle loaves and tiny fish in His hands and pulled off the impossible. The multitudes were sitting along the slopes of the mountain, and those disciples were busy passing out the food to dozens, then hundreds, then thousands!

Remember Philip, who was figuring in minimums? John 6:11 concludes: "as much as they wanted." You can just picture some old fellow who had not eaten for a long time "Hey, Philip, a little more bread over here." So Philip brings the bread—*all they wanted.*

"And when they were filled . . ." (v. 12). That's just like the Lord. Not only does He do the impossible, He does abundantly beyond all anyone could ask or think. He gave to those people until they had plenty. He performed His specialty; He did the impossible.

The river was crossed, the mountain was tunneled, the impossible was accomplished. And to Him, it was as nothing! You'll notice that when the people were filled, He said to the disciples: "Gather up the leftover fragments that nothing may be lost" (v. 12). They gathered them up and filled twelve baskets with fragments from the five barley loaves.

How many disciples? Twelve. How many baskets? Twelve. Can't you picture Philip? He's way down the hill, his basket full. And all the way back up the hill he is saying, "I can't believe it!" It was more than they could ever use. Andrew, the "little thinker," must have been stunned!

Releasing Our Grip

You know the lesson I think the disciples learned, or at least should have learned? *When you face an impossibility, leave it in the hands of the Specialist.* Refuse to calculate. Refuse to doubt. Refuse to work it out by yourself. Refuse to worry or encourage others to worry. Stand against that.

Instead, say, "Lord, I'm carrying around something I cannot handle. Because You are not only able but also willing and anxious, take this off my hands. It's impossible to me, but it is as nothing with You." Persevering through the pressures of impossibilities calls for *that* kind of confidence.

Now, our problem is that we hold on to our problems. If your Swiss watch stops working, you don't sit down at home with a screwdriver and start working on it yourself. You take it to a specialist.

What if you do work on that watch and *then* you take it to a specialist? "Sir, my watch stopped working."

"Oh, really. Let me take a look at it. . . . What in the world have you done to this lovely watch?"

The problem is that the Lord gets all the leftovers. We make all the mistakes and get things tied into nineteen granny knots, then dump it in His lap and say, "Here, Lord."

No! Right at first, say, "It's impossible: I can't handle it. Lord, before I foul it up, it's Yours." He is able to handle it.

I once read an exciting book called *Say It with Love*, by my good friend Dr. Howard Hendricks. You need to read it. In the book he tells the most marvelous true story. I quote:

> We had a lovely couple in Dallas a number of years ago. He sold his business at a loss, went into vocational Christian work, and things got rather rough. There were four kids in the family. One night at family worship, Timmy, the youngest boy, said, "Daddy, do you think Jesus would mind if I asked Him for a shirt?"
>
> "Well, no, of course not. Let's write that down in our prayer request book, Mother."
>
> So she wrote down "shirt for Timmy" and she added "size seven." You can be sure that every day Timmy saw to it

that they prayed for the shirt. After several weeks, one Saturday the mother received a telephone call from a clothier in downtown Dallas, a Christian businessman. "I've finished my July clearance sale and knowing that you have four boys it occurred to me that you might use something we have left. Could you use some boys' shirts?"

She said, "What size?"

"Size seven."

"How many do you have?" she asked hesitantly.

He said, "Twelve."

Many of us might have taken the shirts, stuffed them in the bureau drawer, and made some casual comment to the children. Not this wise set of parents. That night, as expected, Timmy said, "Don't forget, Mommy, let's pray for the shirt."

Mommy said, "We don't have to pray for the shirt, Timmy."

"How come?"

"The Lord has answered your prayer."

"He has?"

"Right." So, as previously arranged, brother Tommy goes out and gets one shirt, brings it in, and puts it down on the table. Little Timmy's eyes are like saucers. Tommy goes out and gets another shirt and brings it in. Out—back, out back until he piles 12 shirts on the table, and Timmy thinks God is going into the shirt business. But you know, there is a little kid in Dallas today by the name of Timothy who believes there is a God in heaven interested enough in his needs to provide boys with shirts.[3]

But we don't usually give God those kinds of chances. We are so totally (and sinfully) confident in ourselves that we don't give God the chance to do what He is a real Specialist at doing. If something is humanly impossible, then what in the world are we doing trying to pull it off?

There's a conclusion to this subject I don't want us to miss. It has to do with "personalizing" what we have been reading about. Because it revolves around a father and his son, it won't be difficult for most of us to identify with it. The man (like many of you) had reached the end of the rope.

Believing the Unbelievable

And they brought the boy to Him. And when he saw Him, immediately the spirit threw him into a convulsion, and falling to the ground, he began rolling about and foaming at the mouth.

And He asked his father, "How long has this been happening to him?" And he said, "From childhood. And it has often thrown him both into the fire and into the water to destroy him. But if You can do anything, take pity on us and help us!"

And Jesus said to him, "'If You can!' All things are possible to him who believes." (Mark 9:20–23)

The only place I know of in the Scriptures where Jesus made that kind of statement is in this passage. The father looked at his son, then turned to Jesus and said "Lord, if You can help. . ." And Jesus said, "'If You can!' Why, I'm a Specialist in that kind of thing. It's impossible with you, but with Me that's nothing."

The father's response is commendable. When he realized his need to trust completely and not fret any longer, he cried out, "I do believe; help me in my unbelief" (v. 24).

Sure enough, some of you who read these words are facing some of the most unbelievable problems anyone could imagine. You've come to the absolute end. There is nothing you can do—zero.

What's God saying to you now? "All things are possible to him who worries"? No. "All things are possible to him who attempts to work it out"? No. "All things are possible to him who *believes.*" The story in Mark 9, of course, is that He saves the boy's life, freeing him from this unclean spirit and providing healing.

The work God wants to accomplish is not going to take place while you sit here reading. It's going to take place when the pressure of impossibility rests upon your shoulders. Child of God, learn a family secret. God specializes in things we think are totally impossible. But being a Gentleman, He won't grab them out of your hands if you insist on holding on to them. "The LORD longs to be gracious to you," says Isaiah. "And . . . He waits on high to have compassion on you" (Isa. 30:18).

Your impossible situation may be a marriage that is almost or altogether on the rocks. It may be a destroyed romance that's left you disillusioned. It may be a terrible habit that you just cannot conquer. It may have to do with your work or your career, or perhaps your schooling. You may be at rock bottom financially. It may be a relationship that is now so strained and pressured that you cannot handle it. If it seems impossible to you, TAKE YOUR HANDS OFF! Ask God, in absolute faith, to take over.

Let me end this chapter with a statement I'd like you to memorize. Really. Before you press on to the next page, commit it to memory. Close the book and repeat it orally several times. It's a statement I say to myself almost every week of my life. It never fails to bring those so-called "impossibilities" into proper focus

> We are all faced with a series of great opportunities brilliantly disguised as impossible situations.

Got any rivers? Any mountains?

6

Waiting: Lingering Test of Patience

Have you heard the American's prayer?

"Lord, give me patience. . . and I want it right now!"

It's awfully hard for a country that exists on frozen dinners, instant mashed potatoes, powdered orange juice, packaged cake mixes, instant-print cameras, and freeway express lanes to teach its young how to wait. In fact, it's next to impossible.

One evening I was fussing about seeds in the grapes my wife had served for supper. After crunching into another seed, I laid down the law. "No more grapes served in the Swindoll home unless they are seedless!" I announced with characteristic dogmatism. Later, when nobody else was around to hear her reproof, Cynthia edged up to me and quietly asked:

"Do you know why seeds in grapes bug you?"

"Sure," I said, "because I bite into those bitter little things and they scatter all over my mouth!"

"No." She smiled. "It's because you're too impatient to dig them out first. The purple grapes really taste better . . . but they take a little more time."

There I stood riveted to the pantry door by a very true (yet painful) set of facts.

I was too busy, too much in a hurry to split open a grape and pull out the seeds. Wow! No wonder waiting is such a difficult hassle for me to handle.

Wouldn't you rather do *anything* than wait? If the truth were known, some of us would rather do the *wrong* thing than wait.

I have found, however, that waiting is the rule rather than the exception in life. The exception is an open door; when you have one—go! They don't happen very often! But waiting when the door is closed doesn't mean you're out of the will of God. You could be right in the center of His will.

The open door is the exception. The bursts of green lights happen just a few seconds in life. The rest of the time is filled with a few yellow lights, and mostly red lights that flash, "Wait, wait, wait!"

Waiting on God is resting instead of worrying. You know you can fake waiting. We all have. We can be all torn up down inside, but we put on that plastic front that says we're at peace when we're really not.

All of this reminds me of a story involving some American soldiers during the Korean War. They had rented a house and hired a local boy to do their housekeeping and cooking. It was common during that war for soldiers to get that kind of setup for easy-come, easy-go, easy-pay.

This little Korean fellow they hired had an unbelievably positive attitude—he was always smiling. So they played one trick after another on him.

They nailed his shoes to the floor. He'd get up in the morning, pull those nails out with pliers, slip on the shoes, and maintain his excellent spirit.

They put grease on the stove handles, and he would wipe each one off, smiling and singing his way through the day.

They balanced buckets of water over the door, and he'd get drenched. But he would dry off and never fuss, time after time.

Finally, they became so ashamed of themselves that they

called him in one day and said, "We want you to know that we're never going to trick you again. Your attitude has been outstanding."

He asked, "You mean no more nail shoes to floor?"

"No more."

"You mean no more sticky on stove knobs?"

"No more."

"You mean no more water buckets on door?"

"No more."

"Okay then, no more spit in soup," he responded with a smile and a shrug.

It's easy to do that, isn't it? We say with our faces that we're waiting, but we're fretting and hiding it. We're "spitting in the soup" more often than not!

A Psalm Encouraging Patience

In Psalm 62 we find a very helpful—and I might add, *simple*—outline to guide our thinking with regard to victorious waiting on the Lord. I don't think we need lengthy teaching on waiting. What we need is long *practice* times! Most of us know *about* it; we need to *do* it more. Let me say just enough on the topic to refresh your memory and get you on your way.

David wrote: "My soul waits in silence for God only" (Ps. 62:1). The literal Hebrew sentence reads almost backwards from the English translation: "Only for God in silence does my soul wait." The word translated "silence" comes from the Hebrew verb that means "to whisper softly." It's the idea of whispering a secret to somebody you love—not loud enough for anyone else to hear. In this case, it's only for God to hear.

Only appears six times in this psalm. For David, there's no one else but the Lord. With this in mind, look carefully at the passage and you'll see what we are to do.

1. Wait for God to direct your steps.

"My soul waits in silence for God only." Don't run ahead. Wait! A red light means "Wait, watch carefully." You can't wait and run at the same time.

Verse 1 is David's declaration; verse 5 is his command. "My soul, wait in silence for God only." He's talking to himself. Ever had to do that? Sure you have, in the growing pains of this Christian life. "Soul, self, listen! You do what you've been told!" That's what the psalmist is saying: "Wait for God to direct your steps."

2. Trust God to provide your needs.

"From Him is my salvation," verse 1 continues. "He only is my rock." Okay, so you are to wait on Him, trusting Him to provide your needs. Now, how are you doing at that? I realize it is old hat; since you were a little child in Sunday school you've heard, "Wait for God to supply your needs." Let me ask, "Have you outgrown that?" I can teach, but I can't "learn you." God must do that, right? And that requires waiting.

My older daughter, Charissa, had an operation on her eye when we lived in Texas. Her eye was weak, and in its weakened condition the muscles caused her eye to turn outward. Our doctor there said, "I'll do my best." When he finished the surgery, her eye was turning in.

We moved to California, and because her eye was not improving, we sought help again. By this time she was having to wear a very heavy lens. We found a pediatric opthalmologist, who worked on nothing but children's eyes. He gave us about the same hope as the Texas physician: "I'll do my best, but now scar tissue has set up. It will be difficult when I get in there. So I want to tell you ahead of time that it could turn all the way in or out in one direction or the other. Just be ready."

As all fathers are, I was convinced that God was going to make everything all right. She came out of surgery bloody, swollen, and bruised. I wanted her to open her eye. I remember standing by the bedside and saying, "Honey, can you open your eye for Daddy? Open it." Her mother and I anxiously awaited that first peek.

Finally, the eye lid came open. The eye was turned all the way in right against her nose! All one could see was the white part of her eye.

I hit bottom!

I'll tell you, that was one of the lowest moments in my life. Honestly, *I did not know how to cope with it.* I said to Cynthia, "I'm going."

"Where are you going?" she asked.

"I don't know," I answered. "I'm just leaving."

I got into the car and drove to my office. I went inside the study, put my "Do Not Disturb" sign on the knob, and locked the doors. My secretary tried to come in, and I told her to go away. It was absolutely dark. I was extremely depressed.

A very close friend talked to my wife and took a chance at finding me in my study. He came by, expressed his genuine concern, and said, "Come on, let's get out of here." He put his arm around me, and we got into his car. He didn't say a lot; we just drove. No sermons and no commands to "snap out of it." Just quietness.

About two or three hours later we went back to the hospital.

"I'm really going to commit this thing to the Lord," he told me. "But we have to wait on Him. We've got to trust Him, Chuck." It was wise counsel from a man I love deeply.

We went back into the hospital to my daughter's room. The night passed. The next morning we looked again at her eye. It was straightening up! When the opthalmologist checked her later and analyzed her condition, he said, "Her fusion is perfect. We'll take her out of glasses." Unto this day her eyesight is perfect.

Now, I don't know why I have never learned that lesson permanently. I guess it's that part of the fallen humanity in me. Have you ever had to learn a lesson twice? Would you believe seven or eight times?

We waited. We could do nothing. There was no one but the Lord to turn to. I had the finest of surgeons who specialized in children's eyes. He warned me. I had to exchange my weakness for God's strength, even though I didn't deserve the exchange. I simply said, "It is impossible, Lord; You do it." And He did.

When we wait for God to direct our steps, He does!

When we trust Him to meet our needs, He will!

What else?

3. Wait silently in stillness.
"My soul waits in silence" (v. 1). "My soul, wait in silence" (v. 5). The hymn writer says:

> Speak, Lord, in the stillness,
> While I wait on Thee;
> Hushed my heart to listen,
> In expectancy.[1]

Some of the best times in prayer are wordless times. I stop speaking, close my eyes, and meditate upon what I have been reading or upon what I have been saying, and I listen inside of myself. I listen deeply. I listen for reproofs. I think of myself as a home with many doors. As I am meditating—and often it helps to close my eyes so I won't be distracted—I unlock doors and open them as I wait. It is here that the Holy Spirit invades. Then, I take circumstances before Him and I listen with doors open.

Please be assured that I have never heard an audible voice. It isn't that kind of answering. It's a listening down inside. It's sensing what God is saying about the situation. His promise is, after all, that He will inscribe His law—His will—upon our hearts and our minds (Heb. 8:10).

It's like what you do when you're in love with a person. Isn't it true—the deeper the love, the less that has to be said? You can actually sit alone together by a fireplace for an hour or two and say very, very little, but it can be the deepest encounter and relationship you know anything about.

Sometime soon take the time to read Revelation 2:1–7. It's a letter Jesus Christ wrote to a group of first-century Christians in a metropolis named Ephesus. Big city, solid saints, strong church—but something was missing.

Do you know what went wrong at Ephesus? They left their first love. They were orthodox and predictable, solid to the core, standing for the truth, but they lost the fire of their love. They fell out of love with Jesus Christ. And the Lord said it was so significant to Him that unless they returned, He'd lift the lampstand from their place and take the light away. They'd be nothing more than another shell with a sign out front, "The Ephesian Church." An empty, stained-glass shell without Christ's warmth.

4. You wait in stability and confidence.
He only is my rock [that's a good word] . . . My stronghold; I shall not be greatly shaken (Ps. 62:2).

There's a sense of stability in trusting the Lord. That's how we wait silently and with a sense of confidence.

Insight on Patience

I love Isaiah 40:31 so much. "Those who wait for the LORD will gain new strength."

In this instance the word wait means "to twist or to stretch in order to become strong." In noun form it means "a line" or "a rope." In other words, it's the idea of stretching or twisting strands of hemp so that, in the process, far greater strength comes.

Someone has called this "the exchanged life," where we trade in our weakness for God's strength. I take my strand (like that of a little spider web) and wrap it around a steel cable of His character (via the waiting process), and then my strand is as strong as His character. I exchange my weakness for His cable-like strength. It never gives way in the heat of the fight; it holds firm.

Those who wait (those who exchange their weakness for His strength) upon the Lord will gain new strength. But remember: The key to the Lord's strength is *waiting*.

Look at the three things the prophet Isaiah says will happen.

They will mount up with wings like eagles,
They will run and not get tired.
They will walk and not become weary. (Isa. 40:31)

The Hebrew meaning is, "They will sprout wings like eagles." Isn't that interesting? What do you think of when you picture a soaring eagle? I think of freedom and strength. I think of dependability of flight. Wouldn't it be great to be able to fly? Those who wait upon the Lord somehow have that option open to them. There is the freedom of flight from life's pressures. And this freedom will be accompanied by inner peace.

Next, Isaiah promises that we who wait will run and not get tired. No longer will we drag an anchor. In this spiritual run a lightness, a fleet-footedness awaits us. Then he says we'll walk and not become weary. Why? Because we're waiting— we're not going in our own strength. We're going in His strength, and God never gets tired. When we wrap our strand around His cable, we can soar in freedom and walk with a light heart.

Benefit of Waiting

Back in Psalm 62, God tells us why we are to wait. It's so simple. It's because:

(a) He is our only *Deliverer.* He is our salvation (v. 1).

(b) He is our only *security.* He is our stronghold (v. 2).

(c) He is our only *hope.* Our hope is from Him (v. 5). What an encouraging statement!

(d) He is our only *glory.* On God my salvation and my glory rests (v. 7). I like that—that's finality.

(e) He is our only *refuge.* My refuge is in God only (v. 7). Only, only, *only* God.

Why wait? Because without Him I don't have deliverance . . . I don't have security . . . I don't have hope . . . I don't have any glory . . . I don't have any refuge. I am *helpless.*

You know what I have finally learned? (I'm a slow learner on some of these things, *á la* the grapes.) I have learned that waiting involves trusting. I have learned that waiting includes praying. I have learned that waiting implies resting. I promise you, God will keep His Word if you are only willing to wait.

Let me remind you of what I told you at the beginning of this book. The key word is *perseverance.* We grow and we learn—not when things come our way instantly—but when we are forced to wait. That's when God tempers and seasons us, making us mellow and mature.

I have read a lot of good stuff about waiting and developing endurance, but I've never read anything better on that subject than J. B. Phillips's paraphrase of James 1:2–4. Please read these closing words very slowly and thoughtfully. After you have finished, pause and pray. Ask the Lord to give you the strength to wait . . . to endure the lingering test of patience.

> When all kinds of trials and temptations crowd into your lives, my brothers, don't resent them as intruders, but welcome them as friends! Realize that they come to test your faith and to produce in you the quality of endurance. But let the process go on until that endurance is fully developed, and you will find you have become men of mature character with the right sort of independence. (James 1:2–4, PHILLIPS)

Let's replace the American's prayer with the Christian's prayer:

Waiting: Lingering Test of Patience

"Lord, make me mature. . .
And I am willing to wait on You."

7

Temptation: Vulnerable Flaw of Weakness

Mark Antony was known as the "silver-throated orator of Rome." He was a brilliant statesman, magnificent in battle, courageous, and strong. And he was handsome. As far as personal qualities are concerned, he could have become a world ruler. But he had the very vulnerable and fatal flaw of moral weakness, so much so that on one occasion his personal tutor shouted into his face, "Oh, Marcus, oh, colossal child! Able to conquer the world, but unable to resist a temptation."

That indictment, I'm afraid, applies not just to Mark Antony, and not just to the people of the unsaved world. If the truth were known, it is applicable to many in the evangelical ranks. We *all* face temptation, and it is a very real fact that many do not yet know how to resist it and overcome it when it appears.

That, very simply, is what I want to deal with here. To write a book on the struggles of the saints without a chapter on temptation would be both unrealistic and incomplete. Why is temptation so "successful"? What makes it work? How can we handle it? Can we learn something that Mark Antony never did—how to resist it?

Trials or Temptations? Knowing the Difference

There's a definite difference between *trials* and *temptations*. Trials are ordeals—tests of our faith. Normally, there is nothing immoral involved in experiencing a trial. A trial is a hardship, an ordeal. But it is generally not something that is evil or brought about by evil.

You will notice that James 1:2–3 addresses the problem of *trials*. "Consider it all joy, my brethren, when you encounter various trials; knowing that the testing of your faith produces endurance."

James goes on through verse twelve writing about trials. But in verse 13 he speaks about *temptation*. "Let no one say when he is tempted, 'I am being tempted by God.'"

Take, for example, Job's trials. He lost his health, his family, his home, his business—he lost everything! But nothing immoral brought about Job's problems; it was a test—in fact, a severe series of tests, as we studied in chapter 4.

Or look at a depressed Elijah under the juniper tree. When his life was threatened, he went away to hide and pleaded with God. "It is enough; now, O LORD, take my life, for I am not better than my fathers" (1 Kings 19:4).

Nothing immoral or evil caused Elijah's experience of depression. It was a test, a hardship, an ordeal.

John (the author of the book of Revelation) was banished to the Isle of Patmos, but not for moral wrongdoing. He was tested by being removed from all that he knew and called dear. It was a trial.

But when we get to temptation, it's different. That is why in James 1:13, the verse includes the word *tempted*. Although it is the same Greek word we have read in verses 1 through 12, in the writer's mind it meant something different. It changed from the idea of an ordeal to the idea of soliciting evil.

A glance at your dictionary will inform you that temptation is "the act of enticement to do wrong, by promise of pleasure or gain." That's right! Temptation motivates you to be bad by promising something good. Isn't that just like the devil?

We tend to think first of the sensual aspect of temptation. If we were to ask, "What is temptation to you?" the vast majority of readers would say, "It is that which is related to the lower nature, the sensual part of life; that which has to do with the lustful eye and the lustful desire of man." That is temptation. But that isn't all of it. We can be tempted to gossip . . . to steal . . . to hold a grudge . . . to lie. There are temptations of every sort. So don't categorize it just in the realm of sensuality, although sensual lust is the most common kind of temptation.

There Is a Simple Answer

Temptation can be counteracted *very definitely by a particular act.* This act is a fruit of the Spirit. In Galatians 5:22–23 we read:

> But the fruit of the Spirit is love, joy, peace, patience, kindness, goodness, faithfulness, gentleness, self-control; against such things there is no law.

The word we are looking for is *self-control.* The Greek word literally means "in strength," and that's exactly what it is. The fruit of the Spirit is inner strength. It is frequently rendered "mastery, or the mastery of self" in extrabiblical literature. In other words, one of the things the Spirit of God promises to do for the child of God is to enable him or her to master self, weaknesses, and areas of temptation. How is temptation counteracted? By *self-control.* Rivet that thought into your head.

But wait a minute. As you read this, you may be tempted to say (as would those who attend the so-called deeper-life conferences), "This isn't something I do; it's something God does. I am not able to do anything. I am only *passively* involved. God is actively involved because, after all, it is the fruit of the Spirit that is self-control."

I'm sure you have heard that kind of thinking. It sounds so right, so profound. But this subtle teaching is in error. Although self-control comes from the Spirit of God, we actively carry it out. Both the Holy Spirit *and we* are active! That's an important thing to remember. It's a team effort, a "both-and" proposition.

There is a teaching floating around today that if something is to be done, I passively wait on God and He does it all. I do nothing—or very little. For me to get involved in it would be something "of the flesh." That sounds so good, so pious. And technically, it is true.

But it's only half the story. That view leaves a person uninvolved in life. In some marvelous process or spiritual ooze, out come all these neat things from my sweet old heart, and I look and marvel at the wonderful work of God, almost as if I'm outside myself watching it happen to me.

Let me tell you, that view is unbiblical—and it doesn't work. If you try to passively deal with temptation, it will conquer you every day of your life! The power and fruit of the Spirit are available; self-control *comes* from God; but I want to say it again: *We carry it out.* Pause and let that sink in.

How do we know this?

The apostle Peter wrote about self-control.

For by these He has granted to us His precious and magnificent promises, in order that by them you might become partakers of the divine nature, having escaped the corruption that is in the world by lust. Now for this very reason also, applying all diligence, in your faith supply moral excellence, and in your moral excellence, knowledge; and in your knowledge, self-control, and in your self-control, perseverance, and in your perseverance, godliness; and in your godliness, brotherly kindness, and in your brotherly kindness, love. (2 Peter 1:4–7)

In that series of commands, the Lord includes *our* responsibility: You supply self-control. Sounds like a contradiction, doesn't it? Paul calls it the "fruit of the Spirit," and it is. Self-control is an ingredient from heaven that God gives us when the Spirit of God lives within and controls us. But Peter said we are to "supply it"!

The alleged contradiction is resolved when we realize that God is the source of the power, and that this means we *pave the way* for it to take place. The same basic supply is given to every child of God, but it is our responsibility to obey and carry out the action of self-control for it to happen in our lives.

Four Facts about Temptation

There are four basic principles regarding temptation. Before we deal with how to handle it, let's get those principles down. They all lie within three verses of James 1.

Let no one say when he is tempted, "I am being tempted by God"; for God cannot be tempted by evil, and He Himself does not tempt anyone. But each one is tempted when he is carried away and enticed by his own lust. Then when lust has conceived, it gives birth to sin; and when sin is accomplished, it brings forth death. (James 1:13–15)

1. Temptation is inevitable.

"Let no one say when he is tempted, 'I am being tempted by God.'" James did not say, "Let no one say, *if* he is tempted. . ." He said, "*When* he is tempted." And there's a difference.

It would be wonderful if we could live without facing temptations. But the simple fact is we cannot. If you think you've found some place, some unique Christian victory secret, some perfect location, some uninhabited island, some ideal church, some area where there is no chance for temptation, don't go there. Because when you do, you're going to spoil it! You see, when you go you take with you your mind—your thoughts—which is the vehicle of temptation. We will never be in a place on earth where there is no temptation. Never.

The monk who lives behind cloistered walls wrestles with temptations as real as the businessman in New York, Chicago, or Los Angeles. The salesman who faces the temptations of competitive life wrestles with allurements no less (and no more) than one who is engaged in the work of Christian ministry. Every one of us faces temptation. It is inevitable. We cannot get away from it.

2. Temptation is never directed by God.

He permits it, to be sure, but He never directs it. God does not direct us into sin. Notice, in James 1:13, that God cannot be tempted by evil, and God does not tempt.

Remember the words of 1 John 1:5: "God is light, and in Him there is no darkness at all." What that means is that God cannot fellowship with sin. He cannot tolerate it, nor does He direct us into it. We sin by our own choice. When the angels surrounded the throne of God in Isaiah 6:3, they rendered to Him the praise of "Holy Holy, Holy, is the Lord of hosts." *Holy* means "totally separate from sin."

Let me say it as carefully as I can: There is nothing wrong with facing temptations. It is not sinful to have tempting things come before us. Hebrews 4:15 tells us that Jesus was "tempted in all things as we are, *yet without sin*" (italics mine).

But how do we react to temptation? "Let no one say when he is tempted, 'I am being tempted by God'" (James 1:13).

Have you ever found yourself doing that? The classic illustration is Adam in the Garden of Eden. When Adam ate of the fruit, and God came and asked, "What is it that you have done?", do you remember what Adam said? "The woman whom Thou gavest to be with me, she gave me from the tree, and I ate." What was he saying? "God, You set me up! Here I was, enjoying the bounty and blessing of the garden, and along came this lady that You brought into my life. And if it hadn't been for her, I wouldn't have been tempted."

That thought is exactly what James wanted to contradict. God is not even *indirectly* engaged in bringing us into sin. To be sure, God certainly permits the events of our lives to take place as they do. But when we yield to the temptations that appear before us, God has had absolutely no part in that act. Instead, it is you and I who have disobeyed and given in to the temptation.

3. Temptation is an individual matter.

"But each one is tempted when he is carried away and enticed by his own lust" (James 1:14). I want you to underscore *each one* and *own*. When we choose to yield to temptation (and we'll deal with that process in just a moment), it is an individual matter. You cannot blame anyone else.

Nothing outside ourselves is strong enough—not even Satan—to cause us to sin. *Sin takes place when we agree to the temptation and follow it.* It takes an agreement on our part. Not until I individually involve myself does sin take place. Up to that point I am safe and pure.

Let me illustrate it this way. I have an attorney friend who works in conjunction with the Federal Reserve Bank in another city. His work involves numerous trips to the Federal Reserve, where stacks and stacks and stacks of currency are kept and counted. If you've never seen it, you can't imagine it!

He made the mistake of taking me there one afternoon. We walked in together and were checked all over. (You know how thorough they are if you've ever been there.) We walked down a narrow hallway and were checked again. We were on closed-circuit security TV cameras all the way. Behind a large section of bulletproof glass (and the construction of the building is such that you cannot get beyond the glass) are people who do nothing but count money. There were numerous stacks of crisp new hundred-dollar bills. He told me there were also stacks of thousand-dollar bills.

I asked him, "How can they stand it behind there?" (revealing something of my own depravity!).

He said, "Everything is fine if they remember their job is only to count pieces of paper. If they begin to concentrate on what those pieces of paper represent, then we have problems."

As long as they are just counting slips of printed paper, that's fine. It could be a stack of magazines or a pile of mail. But if they think, "Hey, this is a spendable hundred-dollar bill I have in my hand!" or "Man, a thousand dollars!"—then they're in for trouble.

Open doors to sin face us all each day. The person centered on Christ and His righteousness says, "Nothing doing," and willfully walks away. The person intent on satisfying his own desires for sin (whether he is a Christian or not) says, "Oh, I just can't help myself," and walks in. The good news for the Christian is that by the power of the Holy Spirit, *we can help it!*

4. Temptation that leads to sin always follows the same overall process. Verse 14 begins the process, and verse 15 carries it out. Pay close attention:

Step 1: The bait is dropped.
Step 2: The inner desire is attracted to that bait.
Step 3: Sin occurs when we yield when we bite the bait.
Step 4: Sin results in tragic consequences we end up hooked and fried.

I'm using these vivid and analogous terms because of James's terminology. Watch what he wrote:

But each one is tempted when he is carried away and enticed by his own lust. Then when lust has conceived, it gives birth to sin; and when sin is accomplished, it brings forth death. (James 1:14–15)

The word *entice* (v. 14) is a fishing term. When you fish, you've got to provide a bait that interests and entices a fish. Fish like shrimp. You put a juicy little shrimp on the hook and try to keep him alive so he keeps snapping and dancing, just as if he's swimming, and you cast out into the ocean. A big gulf trout cannot resist it, if he secs it. If you handle things just right, you've got a sure strike. Why? Because you have chosen a bait that interests the fish.

Here is that fish—safe, casual, doing whatever fish do. Then the bait drops. He has to reckon with it. I don't know how fish think, but they probably look and think something like, "Wow, that looks great!" And when that fish leaves his hiding place for the bait, he's as good as caught.

So are we.

As long as we remain obedient to the Lord, drawing our strength and our delight from Him, the evil system around us can drop all sorts of bait, and it won't seriously interest us. Oh, it's there. But our Lord's Word and power are stronger and more important to us than anything out there.

But when we choose not to obey God and slip out after the bait, we're as good as gone.

Perhaps you're wondering how to say *no* consistently. Look at Genesis 39 for the classic means to handle temptation:

> Now Joseph had been taken down to Egypt; and Potiphar, an Egyptian officer of Pharaoh, the captain of the bodyguard, bought him from the Ishmaelites, who had taken him down there. And the Lord was with Joseph, so he became a successful man. And he was in the house of his master, the Egyptian.
>
> Now his master saw that the Lord was with him and how the Lord caused all that he did to prosper in his hand. So Joseph found favor in his sight, and became his personal servant; and he made him overseer over his house, and all that he owned he put in his charge.
>
> And it came about that from the time he made him overseer in his house, and over all that he owned, the Lord

blessed the Egyptian's house on account of Joseph; thus the Lord's blessing was upon all that he owned, in the house and in the field.

So he left everything he owned in Joseph's charge; and with him there he did not concern himself with anything except the food which he ate. Now Joseph was handsome in form and appearance. And it came about after these events that his master's wife looked with desire at Joseph, and she said, "Lie with me."

But he refused. (Gen. 39:1–8)

Did you notice the bait that was dropped? Here is a handsome single man, alone in Potiphar's home. And Potiphar's wife has a lustful desire for this man and says, "Lie with me." Now, that's what I'd call dropping the bait! Nothing subtle about Mrs. Potiphar! But Joseph refused and look at his answer:

"Behold, with me here, my master does not concern himself with anything in the house, and he has put all that he owns in my charge. There is no one greater in this house than I, and he has withheld nothing from me except you, because you are his wife. How then could I do this great evil, and sin against God?" (Gen. 39:8–9)

Isn't that strong! Here is a man whose heart for *God* took precedence. "How can I sin this way against God?" He consciously and willfully rejected the bait.

And it came about as she spoke to Joseph day after day, [Don't think for a moment that once you have resisted it will end. The same tempting thoughts will come over and over and over. Just because you say no once doesn't mean Satan quits.] that he did not listen to her to lie beside her, or be with her.

Now it happened one day that he went into the house to do his work, and none of the men of the household was there inside. And she caught him by his garment, saying, "Lie with me!" And he left his garment in her hand and fled, and went outside. (Gen. 39:10–12)

I like that! He took off. He ran like mad. She got the garment, and he (eventually) got his reward. By the way, there's a name for folks who linger and try to reason with lust: *victim.*

Practical Ways to Handle Temptations

It can be done! Look, we have made resisting temptation some mystical, unreachable, unattainable talent reserved either for the very old or the very pious. *Baloney!* Saying *no* is something all of us who belong to Christ can do. There's nothing magical about it. You simply put Jesus Christ at the helm of your life and say *NO!*

I think it was John Wesley who said: "Give me men who love nothing but God and hate nothing but sin." That's it precisely. The Lord will give you the power to stand up (or run) and say no when the tempter comes. Let me break this practice down into four workable, practical principles to follow.

1. Counteract temptation. Do not tolerate it.
Paul wrote in Romans 6:13: "Do not go on presenting the

members of your body to sin as instruments of unrighteousness; but present yourselves to God as those alive from the dead, and your members as instruments of righteousness to God."

I see that as an active thing. God does not give us only a negative command. No, He says, "Yield yourself to God." In other words, do not try to peacefully coexist with temptation. Come out against it.

Let's face it: We play around with things that make us weak. Let me get specific. If you are weakened by certain kinds of music, you are playing into the hands of Satan himself to listen to it. If you are weakened by certain motion pictures that bring before your eyes things that build desires within you that you can't handle, then you're not counteracting sin and temptation. You're tolerating it. You're fertilizing it. You're prompting it.

If the newsstand is something you can't handle, stay away from it! If you feed your mind on the garbage of "national magazines" (and I mean even the more popular ones) and cannot handle those things, stay away from them. Quit clucking your tongue and shaking your head as you linger over the pages.

Learn from Joseph. Run!

The words of Dag Hammarskjold—Secretary General to the United Nations in the mid- and late 1950s—throb with wisdom:

> You cannot play with the animal in you without becoming wholly animal, play with falsehood without forfeiting your right to truth, play with cruelty without losing your sensitivity of mind. He who wants to keep his garden tidy doesn't reserve a plot for weeds.[1]

You're a fool, a simpleton, if you *know* what weakens you but feed on it anyway. By constantly bringing temptations before your eyes and letting them sit in your mind, you are playing right into the hand of the devil. If you are weakened by relationships with certain people, abstain from them.

That's not legalism, by the way. It's the marvel of God's grace that He can free you from bondage and enable you to serve Him. Remember what He said? "Do not go on presenting the members of your body to sin" (Rom. 6:13). If that were an impossible feat, God would not say, "Don't keep on doing it. You stop it!"

2. Use the right resistance.
I'll give you some examples, for not all temptations are handled the same in the Scriptures.

When lust or sensual sins are mentioned in the New Testament, we are told to "flee," to run, to get away. That's exactly what Joseph did. If you try to stand and fight it or tolerate it, I guarantee you will ultimately fall victim to it. You may have to make a commitment with your eyes. Do you know there is such a thing?

I have made a covenant with my eyes;
How then could I gaze at a virgin? (Job 31:1)

One of the more popular paraphrases says:

How then could I ogle at a girl? (MLB)

You couldn't put it any more practically. The "eyegate" is a marvel, but it also opens to our experience a whole world of sensuality. When dealing with that kind of temptation, you've got to make that kind of covenant.

The Bible also mentions looking straight ahead and not turning to the right or to the left. See Proverbs 4:25: "Let your eyes look directly ahead, And let your gaze be fixed straight in front of you."

Let me share with you an experience I had in the oriental city of Naha on Okinawa. I used to take a little bus down to the place where a group of men in the military gathered for Bible study. I got off the bus at a particular corner and had to walk about six blocks, since this was as far as the bus would take us. Okinawa was unique—it had more bars per mile than any island in the South Pacific. There was just one sensual opportunity after another along the way. Each joint was an open door to lustful satisfaction.

I discovered that Proverbs 4:25 was literally the answer. I walked straight ahead, looking neither to the right nor to the left.

Moreover, I have discovered that what worked over in Okinawa also works here. When your eyes turn to the right or to the left, you're on your way to grabbing the bait. It is the *second* glance that leads one into sin.

I want to get a little more specific about this. We affect one another in different ways. Women affect men by their looks and by the way they look—by how they dress and the way they look at men.

Men affect women by what they say and by what and how they touch.

Ladies, I am deeply concerned about the way some of you dress. I don't think you fully realize (girls included) how the way you dress affects fellows. I don't care how morally strong a man may be; he still has eyes. And he's got problems with some of you. This is a part of your life that you must answer to before God. I urge each woman reading these lines to realize that your dress and your conduct can be an added temptation of the flesh to men.

And, fellows, guard what you say and how you say it. Also, be careful how and where you touch a woman. You have a responsibility before God to assist in her purity. Hands off!

If you are tempted to gossip and lie, God says there's an answer to that. Avoid it. You say, "Well, that's one way." No, that's the *only* way! A bridle isn't an answer for gossip—you need a muzzle.

Stop talking about them. Say nothing! It is so easy to let those things be said "so we might pray more intelligently." You've heard that one. Or because you're so concerned about them that you feel it's your duty to tell someone about those awful things happening in someone's life.

No, you tell the Lord. He will keep it secret. If it's confidential, if you can't trace the source of the information, if you don't have the okay from the person you are talking about, then keep your mouth shut!

So far we have considered two ways to win the war with temptation: Counteract temptation; don't tolerate it . . . and use the right resistances by fitting the resistance to the attack. But there's another. . .

3. Remind yourself that the final pain will soon erase the temporary pleasure.
That's exactly what Moses did when he chose to walk with God rather than to become absorbed in Egypt's lifestyle.

By faith Moses, when he had grown up, refused to be called the son of Pharaoh's daughter; choosing rather to endure ill-treatment with the people of God, than to enjoy the passing pleasures of sin. (Heb. 11:24–25)

"The passing pleasures of sin." What an eloquent expression—and true! Is sin pleasurable? You bet! It's so pleasurable that people will risk their reputations to taste its flavor. In doing so, all the efforts of our minds to alert us to sin's dangers are neutralized. We turn off the internal warnings as we turn on the desire.

Dietrich Bonhoeffer, a German Lutheran theologian who devotedly loved Jesus Christ, was hanged by the Nazi S.S. Black Guards on April 9, 1945. He was thirty-nine. He had achieved high distinction as a scholar and had won the respect and affection of Christian people in Germany and abroad.

He is gone, but his works survive. His manuscript *Temptation* is one of the best I've ever read on the subject. Bonhoeffer's vivid description of our tendency to turn off the warnings when sin's allurements wink at us needs to be declared to every generation:

In our members there is a slumbering inclination towards desire which is both sudden and fierce. With irresistible power desire seizes mastery over the flesh. All at once a secret, smouldering fire is kindled. The flesh burns and is in flames. It makes no difference whether it is sexual desire, or ambition, or vanity, or desire for revenge, or love of fame and power, or greed for money, or, finally, that strange desire for the beauty of the world, of nature. Joy in God is . . . extinguished in us and we seek all our joy in the creature. At this moment God is quite unreal to us, he loses all reality, and only desire for the creature is real; the only reality is the devil. Satan does not here fill us with hatred of God, but with forgetfulness of God. And now his falsehood is added to this proof of strength. The lust thus aroused envelops the mind and will of man in deepest darkness. The powers of clear discrimination and of decision are taken from us. The questions present themselves: "Is what the flesh desires really sin in this case?" "Is it really not permitted to me, yes— expected of me, now, here, in my particular situation, to appease desire?" The tempter puts me in a privileged position as he tried to put the hungry Son of God in a privileged position. I boast of my privilege against God.

It is here that everything within me rises up against the Word of God.[2]

We've all been there. In order to keep from getting there again, we must tell ourselves over and over, "It will not satisfy! In the end I will have to face unbelievably painful consequences. I will not yield!" Believe me, God will honor your self-control.

4. Control your thought life through the memorized Word.
When the devil launched his full-scale attack against Jesus (Matt. 4:1–11), our Lord withstood temptation by using the Scriptures. "It is written . . . it is written . . . it is written!"
The psalmist asks:

How can a young man keep his way pure?
By keeping it according to Thy word. . . .
Thy word I have treasured in my heart,
That I may not sin against Thee. (Ps. 119:9, 11)

These are familiar but strong words. When the Word of God is stored up in our minds, it stands ready to strike. No weapon can stand against the Truth.

Is this for real? I mean, will it actually work? I can testify by my personal experience that it really does. It *has*, time and again.

I was once in Canada. I had been away from home eight days, and there were two more to go—a weekend. I was lonely and having a pity-party for myself at supper—alone. I bought a newspaper, thumbed through the sports section, and found nothing but hockey—a Canadian favorite but not mine. I heaved a sigh and walked toward the elevator. En route, I heard a couple of young women talking and laughing as they used the hotel phone in the lobby.

I smiled as I passed by and a few steps later punched the "up" elevator button. I got on. So did the two ladies. I punched "6." They didn't reach for the row of buttons, so I asked, "What floor?" One looked at me rather sensually and said, "How about six? Do you have any plans?"

We were all alone on an elevator. In Canada. I was flattered, to be honest, since most folks don't usually mistake me for Tom Selleck. These women were available, and I was lonely. On that trip from the lobby to the sixth floor, I had an extremely significant decision to make . . . the bait had been dropped.

Do you know what immediately flashed into my mind? My wife and four children? No, not at first. My position and reputation? No, not then. The possibility of being seen or set up? No.

God gave me an instant visual replay of Galatians 6:7:

> Do not be deceived, God is not mocked; for whatever a man sows, this he will also reap . . .

and Ephesians 6:11:

> Put on the full armor of God, that you may be able to stand firm against the schemes of the devil . . .

and Romans 6:11–12:

> Even so consider yourselves to be dead to sin, but alive to God in Christ Jesus. Therefore do not let sin reign in your mortal body that you should obey its lusts.

During that elevator lift, the memorized Word flew to my rescue. Right on time.

As I looked back at the two, I replied, "I've got a full evening planned already; I'm really not interested." They looked at me like I was Mork from Ork as I stepped off the elevator (and they stayed on!). I walked to my room, suddenly grateful for the overcoming power of God's Book. As I write these words to you, I am filled with renewed strength because His Word has kept me faithful again and again for forty years of marriage. Yes, the memorized Word works.

In a quaint little village north of Pittsburgh, Pennsylvania, a shining new red brick building was built, designed to be the new city hall. It also housed the police and fire departments. It was a small building, but the people loved it.

In a matter of just a few months, however, the building began to show some obvious cracks. The windows would not close all the way. Before too many weeks, the doors were ajar and would not shut. The floor buckled. Finally, the sidewalk in front of the building cracked. In a period of less than a year, the building had to be condemned.

A careful, expensive investigation was made, and it was found that deep below the surface they had built too near some mining work. The mining had weakened the foundational area, so that slowly but surely, this building was cracking, shifting, sinking, dropping, and breaking into pieces because of a flaw underneath.

The moral of this isn't difficult to grasp. If you mess around with temptation long enough, playing with it, lingering near its bait over and over and over again, then down in the heart and life of your character there will be permanent damage. That vulnerable flaw or weakness will lead to serious moral damage that you cannot imagine.

Come to terms with this now . . . or you will regret it later.

PART II
Internal Affairs

8
Mistakes: Inevitable Marks of Imperfection

We Christians suffer from a very common ailment: making honest mistakes. I'm not talking now about willful sin. Mistakes can *lead* into sin, but honest mistakes are simple . . . well, let's listen to Mr. Webster.

To make a mistake means "to choose wrongly," or "to make a wrong judgment." Webster amplifies this in a second meaning: "a wrong attitude, action, or statement proceeding from faulty judgment, inadequate knowledge or intention." Remember now, we're not talking about out-and-out purposeful rebellion. We're certainly not talking about demonic deception. We're talking about honest-to-goodness, simple garden-variety mistakes to which we are all prone. But these simple mistakes (as we shall see) frequently open the door to sinful activity.

I have found five categories of mistakes illustrated in Scripture. Our mistakes, and some of the factors leading to those mistakes, are in these categories.

1. Panic-Prompted Mistakes

These are mistakes we invariably make out of *fear*, or from being in a *hurry*, or as a result of *worry*. We panic and make a wrong decision.

Look at Genesis 12:10. This mistake was made by Abraham.

Remember that God had said to Abraham, "You are my man. Through you a nation will be born, and you will have a heritage like no other man that has lived, Abraham. Stand fast. Trust Me through all the cares of life, and I will bring through your life a nation."

With that promise still ringing in his ears, Abraham panicked. We read: "Now there was a famine in the land." There was no bread and no meat. Apparently, there was not much water either. Things had gotten tight. So Abraham made a mistake and went down to Egypt.

Why? He got shook. Even though God had said, "Abraham, you stay beside Me at the altar at Bethel, and I will make you a man of God, and through you I'll give birth to a nation," he panicked and headed south, for the famine was severe.

And when you make a "panic mistake," you simply make the first one, and it quickly leads to the next, like a row of dominoes. Enter *the next!*

> And it came about when he came near to Egypt, that he said to Sarai his wife, "See now, I know that you are a beautiful woman; and it will come about when the Egyptians see you, that they will say, 'This is his wife'; and they will kill me, but they will let you live. Please say that you are my sister so that it may go well with me because of you, and that I may live on account of you." (Gen. 12:11–13)

Oh, *we* know that whether he will live or not doesn't depend on Sarah; he will live on account of God. But you see, when you move into Panic Palace, your whole focus gets twisted, and you forget what God has said. Instead, you give direct attention to what man has said (rather than God) and what people think (rather than Scripture).

Numbers 13 and 14 illustrate a second example of panic errors. The Hebrew spies went into the Promised Land to see if the children of Israel could take the country just beyond Kadesh Barnea, a border city. The spies came back with a U.S. Supreme Court sort of majority report. Ten said, "No way! There are giants in the land. Compared to them we're like little grasshoppers." Two of them said, "We can take that land. God gave it to us. It's a *promised* land!"

The people believed the majority report out of panic fear. They determined not to go into the land. And what happened? They were made to wander in the wilderness for forty years. They made a *bad* mistake; in this case it was out-and-out sin. But what prompted it was the mistake of listening to wrong counsel . . . and believing it.

I find that for us moderns, panic-prompted mistakes often have to do with two major issues: romance and finance.

Can't you hear the young woman saying, "I've come to that ripe old age of twenty-four and still haven't found a mate"? I know a number of people who are thirty-four and would be happy to trade off with her, because in panic they raced ahead of God and got themselves a mate. They wish they were back at age twenty-four now, unscarred and still available.

The matter of finances is an equally familiar problem. In panic we grab the first lifesaver loan we can get hold of. Before going down for the third time in a sea of debt, we just sort of bubble out, "Where are you, Lord? . . . ord? . . . d? . . . ? . . ."

If you are on one of those two precipices, *sit tight. Stand fast.* God knows what He is doing.

2. "Good-Intentioned" Mistakes

Now, in a sense, all mistakes are like this if they are genuine mistakes. But let's categorize this one by itself: "good-intentioned" mistakes. This is a mistake that is made ignorantly *with an absolutely pure motive.* You have good intentions, but you use the wrong planning or the wrong method.

Consider Moses in Exodus 2. He's forty years old. (You never get to the place, even in the Bible, where you're too old to make mistakes!) Middle-aged Moses realizes he is potentially able to deliver His people from the bondage of Egypt. So he rolls up his sleeves and, preempting Frank Sinatra by some 3,500 years, says, "I'll do it my way."

> Now it came about in those days, when Moses had grown up, that he went out to his brethren and looked on their hard labors; and he saw an Egyptian beating a Hebrew, one of his brethren. So he looked this way and that, and when he saw there was no one around, he struck down the Egyptian and hid him in the sand. (Exod. 2:11–12)

With the right motive (delivering the Hebrew, avenging the oppressed), he killed a man. After all, shouldn't he defend his Hebrew brother? His blood was Hebrew even though his whole culture was Egyptian. His desire was to defend what was right, but his good intentions led to tragedy: the sin of murder.

And you know what? He thought everybody would understand. That's another characteristic, by the way, of good-intentioned mistakes. You have the feeling that "everybody will understand." But look at Acts 7. It's the same story about Moses but told 1,500 years later from a different vantage point:

But when he was approaching the age of forty, it entered his mind to visit his brethren, the sons of Israel. And when he saw one of them being treated unjustly, he defended him and took vengeance for the oppressed by striking down the Egyptian. *And he supposed that his brethren understood that God was granting them deliverance through him; but they did not understand.* (Acts 7:23–25, italics mine)

I'm not a prophet, but I've made enough mistakes in my life to be somewhat of an expert on the subject. With good intentions, you can plunge ahead and roll up your sleeves and do things in the flesh—and they will come back to haunt you. It's as if we decide to do *God's* will *our* way. Know what? That's *not* God's will! I remember one time I was leading a Bible study group, somewhat like a seminar. We were sitting in a circle, and I suppose there were twenty people there. A couple of chairs were empty, and a fellow came to the door with a woman who appeared to be twenty years his senior. "You and your mother can sit right here," I said.

Wouldn't you know, it was his wife!

They left at the first coffee break. Friends and neighbors, I could have cut my tongue out. I had good intentions, but I didn't think.

3. Negligent Mistakes

Men, we suffer from this one especially—passive, negligent mistakes. They occur in Scripture rather often, relating to the home, to the role of a father. Negligent mistakes are a result of laziness or oversight or inconsistency or just a plain lack of discipline.

Let me show you an illustration, and maybe you'll be shocked. (If I were just getting started in the Scripture, I would be shocked.) The man is David. In 1 Kings 1:5–6 we read:

> Now Adonijah the son of Haggith exalted himself, [Haggith was David's wife—one of many, by the way. If you study the genealogy of David, you'll discover that this man was grossly guilty of polygamy. I count eighteen wives; there might well have been more. Some of those are not even named, but one of them was Haggith, the mother of Adonijah] saying, "I will be king." So he prepared for himself chariots and horsemen with fifty men to run before him.
> And his father had never crossed him at any time by asking,
> "Why have you done so?"

Passive negligence.

Adonijah was born a rebel, grew up a rebel, and when he reached the "age of accountability" he refused to be accountable! He rebelled, saying, "I'll become king." Part of the problem was a father who never crossed the son. David never said to his son, "Son, you've got a bent toward rebellion. As your father, I am responsible before God to curb that bent, to deal with it until you yourself can get it under control."

No, David was like many dads. Too busy. Preoccupied. And therefore, negligent. It's a common mistake among successful, high-achieving fathers.

Benjamin Franklin once wrote these insightful words:

> A little neglect may breed mischief: for want of a nail the

shoe was lost; for want of a shoe the horse was lost; and for want of a horse the rider was lost.[1]

That's the way negligence is.

4. Unrestrained-Curiosity Mistakes

Of all the five categories of mistakes, this is probably the most attractive to young people, although it is not exclusively their problem. Unrestrained curiosity usually relates to the sensational or the demonic.

The whole world of curiosity is in one sense a very creative part of our lives, but we are destined for trouble if curiosity is not restrained.

First Samuel 28 is the story of a king who had lost both his confidence and his power. When his friend Samuel died, King Saul sought to speak to Samuel through a spiritualist medium. He disguised himself and, taking two other men with him, he paid a visit to a woman seer by night. They purchased a contract with the netherworld, and before long they were in touch with the other world. It began as unrestrained curiosity—a costly mistake. It led to a horrible sin that ultimately became part of the cause of Saul's death (1 Chron. 10:13–14).

5. Blind-Spot Mistakes

These are the ones we repeat most often, the ones we commit out of ignorance or habit or even poor parental influence.

We're blinded to the truth, and we stumble into this kind of thing time after time.

The last part of Acts 15 is the account of a conflict between two godly men, Paul and Barnabas. John Mark, Paul's earlier companion, had deserted him in the previous missionary journey. When they got ready to take the next missionary journey, the apostle Paul was discussing matters with Barnabas, who suggested they take John Mark with them. "No way!" said Paul.

In Paul's mind, John Mark was not profitable to him. Paul considered him a shipwreck, a fluke, a failure. He had a blind spot when it came to that weakness in other people. So he made a mistake. (Later in his ministry he was man enough to admit that Mark was profitable to him—See 2 Tim. 4:11.)

There is perhaps an even clearer example of this kind of mistake in Galatians 2:11–15. There's no need to go into any great depth of study; we just need to see the issue. Peter (called "Cephas" in the Galatians passage) had a blind spot when it came to the question of grace, especially as it related to his diet.

When he was around Jews, he ate good ole kosher cookin'. But when the Gentiles were there he'd stuff down the ham sandwiches and pigs feet like they were going out of style. He really couldn't let himself enjoy the full benefits of grace . . . but worse than that, he fell into a hypocritical lifestyle, doubtlessly justifying both the legalism and the liberty whenever necessary.

A mistake! Paul saw through it immediately and "opposed him to his face." Peter's response is not recorded, but one has little difficulty imagining his embarrassment. It is remarkable how blind-spot mistakes can be so obvious to everyone but the victim!

Of all the mistakes we make, this is the one we rationalize

the most. We could probably pass a lie detector test because we are so *convinced* that we did the right thing.

A Psalm of Balm—for the Mistaken

Psalm 31 was written, I believe, on a blue day in David's life. As we look at this psalm, we're going to see that he was broken and disappointed. He most likely wrote it on the heels of a mistake, maybe one he had made out of panic. Maybe it was one that was related to his home. Perhaps shortly after having a blind spot pointed out, he said:

> In Thee, O LORD, I have taken refuge;
> Let me never be ashamed;
> In Thy righteousness deliver me.
> Incline Thine ear to me, rescue me quickly;
> Be Thou to me a rock of strength,
> A stronghold to save me.
> For Thou art my rock and my fortress;
> For Thy name's sake Thou wilt lead me and guide me. . . .
> Into Thy hand I commit my spirit. (Ps. 31:1–3, 5)

Familiar words? Sure, those last six were Jesus' very words as He was dying on Calvary. Just before He gave up His spirit, He said to God, "To You I commit My spirit." It was the lowest point, physically and emotionally, in the entire life of the Messiah. But let's apply all this to our post-mistake depression periods in life.

You'll discover, after the grave and painful ramifications of making a mistake, that it is only to God that you can commit your spirit at that time. No other person can give the comfort you need. On the heels of a mistake, get on your knees, fall before God, and lay out your shame and humiliation. No one else can heal you of that sense of shame and self-disappointment. The old songwriter was right: "No one understands like Jesus"—no one.

Now, from that perspective, let us observe how God views us when we've made those mistakes.

> I hate those who regard vain idols;
> But I trust in the Lord.
> I will rejoice and be glad in Thy lovingkindness,
> Because Thou hast seen my affliction;
> Thou hast known the troubles of my soul. (Ps. 31:6–7).

First, God views us *realistically*. It is very helpful and important to remember that God sees us as we really are. We work so hard sometimes to keep the full truth from other people, for fear they will not understand. We burn up all kinds of emotional energy keeping our real selves from one another.

Mark Twain once wrote: "Everyone is a moon, and has a dark side which he never shows to anybody."[2] But God knows that dark side. He sees it plainly.

David said, "I rejoice, because You are realistic, Lord, when You see me. You know my bents. You know my tendencies. You know my sense of panic, my fears. You know how I was reared. You know the bad habits I have picked up. You know my track record. You also know my intentions, not just my actions. You have seen my affliction."

The second thing I notice about God is that He views us *thoroughly*. "Thou hast seen my affliction; Thou hast known the troubles of my soul" (Ps. 31:7). I wonder if that was the place that old Negro spiritual got its start—"Nobody knows the trouble I seen, nobody knows but Jesus. . . ."

You see, afflictions have to do with the externals. Troubles have to do with the internals. "Lord, You see the whole world of affliction and You feel with me the trouble down inside." Remember that great statement regarding our Savior's understanding heart? "For we do not have a high priest who cannot sympathize with our weaknesses" (Heb. 4:15).

There is great comfort in those words! But have you ever read two verses *before* that one? Verse 13 says that nothing is hidden from God's sight. Everything is laid bare to His eyes—and still He sympathizes with us! I'll tell you, that fills me with encouragement. Afflicted without and troubled within, mistake-prone though we are, He understands!

Seeing us realistically, seeing us thoroughly—how does He treat us? "Thou has not given me over into the hand of the enemy" (Ps. 31:8).

He does not reject us! That's the thing we fear the most, I believe, when we've made a mistake. If it's been a bad mistake, we especially fear divine rejection. We're afraid God is going to say, "That's it! Go to your room! Finished!" But David said:

> Thou hast not given me over into the hand of the enemy; [and I love this part] Thou hast set my feet in a large place. (Ps. 31:8)

That doesn't mean he had big feet. It means God gave him room. He doesn't crowd us. He gives us space.

Ever notice that when you try to find relief, people crowd you? They tighten the rope. They put very stringent limitations on you. They put a time limit on you or some other reminder of obligation. David said in this verse, "Lord, You have a large place; You give me space; You give me room."

I want you to know that our heavenly Father is not anxious. He is quietly at ease and is calm while you are coming to your senses. He knows what He is doing. Isn't that a relief? It makes trusting Him so much easier. No wonder David said: "But as for men, I trust in Thee, O LORD" (v. 14).

How does He instruct us at those times?

1. He instructs us in a context of trust, not suspicion.
"I trust You, Lord." When you turn your situation over to man, there will often be suspicion that you will make the mistake again. Man will be there with seventeen warnings, six sermons, two songs, and a poem to back them up—and a long, long index finger driving itself into your chest, saying. "You'd better watch that." God instructs us in a context of trust, not suspicion.

2. God instructs us in all of life, not just the pleasant times.
Are you ashamed, embarrassed, humiliated, failing, losing? Your times are in His hands. He is instructing you in the bad times just as He does in the pleasant times. That's why James says, "Don't resent them [corrections] as intruders, but welcome them as friends" (James 1:2, PHILLIPS).

3. God instructs us in the secret places, not the public places.

> How great is Thy goodness,
> Which Thou hast stored up for those who fear Thee,
> Which Thou has wrought for those who take refuge in Thee.
> Thou dost hide them in the secret place of Thy presence
> from the conspiracies of man. (Ps. 31:19–20)

The best things we learn from mistakes are learned in secret, for it is there He tells us His secrets, and in doing so, covers us with His love and understanding.

"Christians are not perfect, just forgiven" is one of the many bumper stickers we've seen. Frankly, I'm not too big on most of the stuff folks stick on their cars, but that one I like.

It came in handy recently . . . not on my car, but on the one weaving in and out of heavy freeway traffic last week. The guy was obviously late and irritated as he began to tailgate my car. I changed lanes so he could pass, and he darted into the space on my left.

At precisely the same time, another car shot into that same lane in front of him, and instead of plowing into that car, the speedy stranger pulled over in front of *me*—fast. I slammed on my brakes, almost got rear-ended, and barely missed his car—at fifty-five miles per hour!

Just then, he looked in his rearview mirror and hunched down in his seat, embarrassed. I glanced at his bumper sticker and smiled down inside. It was perfect timing!

He backed off his breakneck pace, and I soon pulled up even with his car. I looked over at him and suddenly realized he was one of our church members. (He had recognized me earlier in his mirror.) I rolled down my window, smiled, and yelled across the freeway—"You're forgiven, remember?" Relieved, he returned my smile.

Yes, not even becoming a Christian erases our imperfections. We still make mistakes—even dumb mistakes. But, thank God, forgiveness gives us hope. We still need a lot of it.

▮9
Inferiority: Contagious Plague of Self-Doubt

A man paid a visit to his local psychologist. When the doctor asked him what had prompted the visit, the man said, "I'm suffering from an inferiority complex."

In the ensuing weeks, the psychologist put his new patient through an intensive battery of tests. Next came the long wait while the test results were tabulated and appropriate correlations were made.

Finally, the doctor called the man and asked him to return to the clinic. "I have some interesting news for you," the doctor began.

"What's that?" asked the man.

"It's no complex," the psychologist retorted. "You *are* inferior."

Certainly there is no question that some of us have infinitely more to feel inferior about than others. Abraham Lincoln was wrong: All men are *not* created equal when it comes to various mental—and physical—capabilities. But we do have far more natural endowments than most of us will ever need.

For example, did you know that there is enough atomic power in one human body to destroy the city of New York? A brilliant scientist several years ago told me some astounding facts concerning the power of the human mind. He said, "It is almost impossible to calculate this phenomenon, but as best as I can figure it, if we could build an electronic computer that could do all the human mind could do, it would be a building about a city block wide and deep and twenty-two stories high." Today that same human mind could reduce that huge computer to credit card size for your wallet!

The power of the human body and mind is nothing short of incredible. Yet, in spite of this, many people cower in timidity and inferiority. Before we look at the lives of three men in Scripture—two who had the problem and did not conquer it, and one who could have had the problem but did not cultivate it—let us make a few general observations about an inferiority complex.

Some Helpful Observations

First of all, inferiority feelings are not necessarily related to intelligence. Interesting studies have been done on human behavior as it relates to intelligence. Often those who were highly intelligent—130 IQ and above—suffered from more inferior feelings than those beneath that mark! In fact, they suffered a great deal more than the others. And those who had a relatively low intelligence quotient often had relatively few problems with feelings of inferiority.

A second observation is that an inferiority complex is not always noticed on the surface. People usually mask it in a number of interesting ways.

A common cover-up is adopting the personality type we frequently call the superiority complex—the boisterous type of person who seems always on top of things. These people frequently have inferior self-images, but you wouldn't catch it on the surface.

Another mask is that of sarcasm. A sarcastic manner is often nothing more than a cover-up or a compensation for inferiority feelings.

A third observation, or clarification, is that this is certainly not unique to the non-Christian world. We Christians wrestle with the problem just as much, or perhaps even a bit more, than non-Christians.

I am acquainted with a man who played professional basketball for the Boston Celtics. He was not on the starting five, but he was an excellent substitute—probably number six or seven—and played in nearly every game. He was in a church I served years ago in Waltham, Massachusetts.

I will never forget asking him on one occasion to lead in prayer. He is a born-again man and certainly has a witness for Christ. But I have never seen a person struggle like that man struggled to lead in public prayer. And it was not in a big church meeting; it was just a small group gathering.

Shortly after the meeting ended, he said to me, "Hey, come here, Chuck."

I walked over to him. "Yes?"

He said quietly, "Would you mind not doing that again?" Beads of perspiration covered his forehead. His neck was red all around his collar. He really was distressed. He went on to tell me that he suffered from inferiority feelings, that he was working on it, but was just not very far down the road. Candidly, I was shocked. This NBA star was good-looking, big, popular, and multitalented. His inferiority was the best-kept secret in the church!

I have another young friend in mind who graduated from Dallas Seminary. He was an intern at a church I once pastored. He was an absolute animal on a basketball court! But when he walked off the court, all of that left. While he was in his element playing the game, you couldn't touch him. He was tall, aggressive, and well coordinated. As I recall, he had been the team captain at a West Coast college. But in the normal routine of life, he just slipped away out of sight so people wouldn't see him. (By the way, he has since done a great job of conquering his problem of inferiority.)

It isn't always obvious on the surface. You see people everywhere—from military personnel to pro athletes—who find very great comfort and ease in doing their work *behind* the scenes, but who cannot handle face-to-face contact with other people. Inferiority is a hidden beast in many a breast.

My good friend Dr. James Dobson has written a splendid book on this problem entitled *Hide or Seek*. In it he relates the true story of a bright young seminary student who wrote Dr. Dobson a letter while the noted psychologist was lecturing at the school. As they finally met each other face to face, the troubled seminarian stood with tears streaming down his cheeks and openly declared gross feelings of inadequacy. An administrator of the seminary later told Dr. Dobson the young man was the last person in the student body of three hundred he would ever have expected to feel that way.[1]

And then an event far more tragic than that occurred on the campus.

Sitting in the audience that same day was another student with the same kind of problems. However, he did not write me a letter. He never identified himself in any way. But three weeks after I left, he hanged himself in the basement of his apartment. One of the four men with whom he lived called long distance to inform me of the tragedy. He stated, deeply shaken, that the dead student's roommates were so unaware of his problems that he hanged there five days before he was missed![2]

Three Biblical Candidates for an Inferiority Complex

Moses

With the previous observations in mind, let's look at a young man—eighty years of age (that's meant as a compliment so no one will feel inferior about their age!). You would certainly not expect Moses to be suffering from inferiority feelings, but he was. He felt inferior because he had a background of failure. Guilt frequently does breed inferiority. It may be something you have done or something you feel can never be righted, and you resign yourself to live out your life with that weight of failure resting heavily on your shoulders.

This is Moses when we find him in Exodus 3. He murdered a man in Egypt. Then he left Egypt and was tucked away in an unfamiliar area known as the Midian Desert in a place of obscurity. He was living with his father- and mother-in-law, and, with his wife, was raising a family of three children. So he had been forgotten . . . for forty years he had not even been seen by his people in Egypt. Riveted into his head were deeply rooted feelings of inferiority. You may recall the story in Exodus 3:1–10:

> Now Moses was pasturing the flock of Jethro his father-in-law, the priest of Midian; and he led the flock to the west side of the wilderness, and came to Horeb, the mountain of

God. And the angel of the Lord appeared to him in a blazing fire from the midst of a bush; and he looked, and behold, the bush was burning with fire, yet the bush was not consumed. So Moses said, "I must turn aside now, and see this marvelous sight, why the bush is not burned up."

When the Lord saw that he turned aside to look, God called to him from the midst of the bush, and said, "Moses, Moses!" And he said, "Here I am."

Then He said, "Do not come near here; remove your sandals from your feet, for the place on which you are standing is holy ground. . . ." And the Lord said, "I have surely seen the affliction of My people who are in Egypt, and have given heed to their cry because of their taskmasters, for I am aware of their sufferings. So I have come down to deliver them from the power of the Egyptians, and to bring them up from that land to a good and spacious land, to a land flowing with milk and honey. . . . And now, behold, the cry of the sons of Israel has come to Me; furthermore, I have seen the oppression with which the Egyptians are oppressing them. Therefore, come now, and I will send you to Pharaoh, so that you may bring My people, the sons of Israel, out of Egypt."

I'm convinced of this: All Moses heard was, "I send YOU." That's all he had to hear. Immediately, that eighty-year-old saint began to think of how unworthy, unstable, and faltering he had been. For forty years he had nursed the image of himself: "a failure." He didn't feel capable of that task

Now, we're not reading about humility; it's inferiority. To feel inferior is *not* to be humble. Humble people, of all the people on the face of the earth, have the highest degree of confidence in God—a quiet, self-assuring inner confidence that God is going to do what He says He will do.

While doing some biblical research recently on the subject of humility and servanthood, I came across a remarkable statement Paul made twice to the Corinthians. In a context of the importance of humility he writes: "For I consider myself not in the least inferior to the most eminent apostles" (2 Cor. 11:5).

And he repeats that strength in the next chapter (12:11). No, humility does not suggest inferiority. But look how Moses responded in Exodus 3:11: "Who am I, that I should go to Pharaoh, and that I should bring the sons of Israel out of Egypt?"

He questioned God. He was really saying, "I can't go; I'm not qualified." This called into question both God's power and His ability to select leadership, for the Lord promised His presence:

> Certainly I will be with you, and this shall be the sign to you that it is I who have sent you: when you have brought the people out of Egypt, you shall worship God at this mountain. (Exod. 3:12)

Now you might think that Moses suddenly believed God, quickly took the task in hand, and shoved off for Egypt. But he didn't. Look at 4:1.

Then Moses answered and said, "What if they will not believe me or listen to what I say?

Where were Moses' eyes right then? On himself. He was saying, "I mean, when I get in front of them and come out with this business of 'There's going to be a deliverance,' what if they won't believe me? What if they doubt that You even spoke to me?"

So the Lord replied in 4:2–3:

"What is that in your hand?" And he said, "A staff."
Then He said, "Throw it on the ground." So he threw it on the ground, and it became a serpent.

Here is the power of God. "Get your eyes off yourself, Moses. If I can turn a rod into a serpent and then turn that serpent back into a rod, I can change the heart of Pharaoh." God was convinced Moses was the man.
But Moses wasn't convinced.

The LORD said to Moses, "Stretch out your hand and grasp it by its tail"—so he stretched out his hand and caught it, and it became a staff in his hand—"that they may believe that the LORD, the God of Abraham, the God of Isaac, and the God of Jacob, has appeared to you." (Exod. 4:4–5)

But Moses still resisted placing his confidence in the Lord.

Then Moses said to the LORD, "Please, Lord, I have never been eloquent, neither recently nor in time past, nor since Thou has spoken to Thy servant; for I am slow of speech and slow of tongue." (4:10)

Can you identify with Moses as you read verse 10? How frequently one hears from others, "Now, don't ask me to do that, because I really can't speak very well." Or, "I'm not a person who knows how to handle myself on my feet." Moses is playing the "I'm-just-a-simple-man" game.
This always interests me. An inferiority complex is a satanic deception that keeps numbers of young people from considering vocational Christian service. Whether it is as a missionary or a

minister they think they have to be eloquent. They think they have to be witty and quick-tongued.

In no uncertain terms, God told Moses he did not have to be eloquent.

> "Who has made man's mouth? Or who makes him dumb or deaf, or seeing or blind? Is it not I, the LORD?" (4:11)

God was saying, "I take full responsibility. I'm responsible. I made your tongue."

Then He made a most encouraging promise: "Now then go, and I, even I, will be with your mouth, and teach you what you are to say" (4:12).

God will take your inabilities and change them, giving you the words to say. Disabilities need not disqualify.

Look, if you feel inferior with your tongue and with your words, God is able to handle that inability and turn what seems to be a restraint or barrier into something that is a blessing if for nothing more than to keep you trusting Him from word to word.

Jeremiah

We often have the idea that God's prophets never had feelings of inferiority or inadequacy. But Jeremiah certainly did.

Here again is a man who was not simply humble, but a man who felt inferior. I am using as a reference here Jeremiah 1:4–5:

> Now the word of the LORD came to me saying, "Before I formed you in the womb I knew you, and before you were born I consecrated you; I have appointed you a prophet to the nations."

And when Jeremiah heard those words, his response was: "Alas, Lord GOD! Behold, I do not know how to speak, Because I am a youth" (Jer. 1:6).

That's the same thing Moses said! Why is it that as soon as God places His hand on a person, he will usually say, "I can't preach." Is that the *only* way God uses people? You can just hear Jeremiah's knees knocking, as he said, "I am a youth . . . I'm too young!" He knew he would be sent to the elders of the land, and he didn't have that superstar charisma, that winsome wisdom that would reach them and win them by the thousands.

> But the LORD said to me, "Do not say, 'I am a youth,' Because everywhere I send you, you shall go, And all that I command you, you shall speak." (Jer. 1:7)

How is that for strong medicine?

> "Do not be afraid of them, For I am with you to deliver you." (Jer. 1:8)

Isn't it curious that we frequently have feelings of inferiority because of a *fear of that other person?* God puts His finger on it, and says, "Jeremiah, don't be afraid of them. I am with you to deliver you. Don't be afraid." The marvelous story is found in 1:9:

> Then the LORD stretched out His hand and touched my mouth, and the LORD said to me, "Behold, I have put My words in your mouth."

That isn't just idle prattle. It actually happens. If you're going to speak God's message, you're going to speak God's words. He will place His words—not yours—in your mouth.

Someone has said that the real difference between the preacher of the flesh and the one who speaks from the Spirit is that the preacher of the flesh has to say something, while the one who speaks from the Spirit has something to say. Jeremiah had something to say. He spoke God's words. And inferiority would have nullified Jeremiah's impact.

Amos

Now let's consider a man who is not well known today. His name is Amos. I want you to appreciate Amos because he was a man who was not like the cultured Isaiah or Daniel or Ezekiel. He didn't have formal academic training. Here was a man who had every reason to feel inferior. I take it that he was not attractive. He didn't dress well. He certainly was not eloquent. He had not been raised among royalty, as had Solomon.

Do you know what he did for a living? He was a fig-picker. That's right! He was a picker of sycamore fruit. Sycamore fruit is a lot like the fig. The picker also has the responsibility of mashing the fruit so it will be soft for the buyer. And when you mash the sycamore fruit, you stain your hands.

So here is a fellow whose background is a fig-picker or, if you prefer, a fig-squeezer. Can you see those credentials on the dossier of, say, an Episcopal bishop, or the pastor of First Presbyterian Church, or a scholarly prof at an evangelical seminary! Seriously, I do wonder how many great people like Amos are lost to God's service today for lack of "good credentials."

When we pick up the scene, Amos is standing in the king's

court. In fact, he and the official representative of the king are eyeball-to-eyeball. Amos is in his old, rough garments, standing there preaching. Now read Amos 7:10–11:

> Then Amaziah, the priest of Bethel, sent word to Jeroboam, king of Israel, saying, "Amos has conspired against you in the midst of the house of Israel; the land is unable to endure all his words. For thus Amos says, 'Jeroboam will die by the sword and Israel will certainly go from its land into exile.'"

That was his message! Not much comfort there. Here is the priest: polished, exquisite, beautifully attired, eloquent, jeweled, (unsaved!), standing before scrubby Amos with his stained hands and frowning face.

> Then Amaziah said to Amos, "Go, you seer, flee away to the land of Judah, and there eat bread and there do your prophesying!" (Amos 7:12)

Can't you see him? "Get out! Scram! Move!"

> Then Amos answered and said to Amaziah, "I am not a prophet, nor am I the son of a prophet; for I am a herdsman and a grower of sycamore figs. But the LORD took me from following the flock and the LORD said to me, 'Go prophesy to My people Israel.'" (Amos 7:14–15)

Where were Amos's eyes? On the Lord. Amos didn't ask for this job; God called him. The Lord said to him, "Go prophesy to My people Israel."

He continued:

"And now hear the word of the LORD; you are saying, 'You shall not prophesy against Israel nor shall you speak against the house of Isaac.'

"Therefore, thus says the LORD, 'Your wife will become a harlot in the city [that's not any way to win friends, I can assure you], your sons and your daughters will fall by the sword, your land will be parceled up by a measuring line, and you yourself will die upon unclean soil. Moreover, Israel will certainly go from its land into exile.'" (Amos 7:16–17)

This is a crazy thought, but you know what came to my mind when I thought of Amos and this priest Amaziah trying to converse? It would be like hearing a duet sung by Maria Callas and Tiny Tim. You could never mix those voices. And when you put these two ancient characters together, they don't fit either.

Yet Amos doesn't back down a bit. He says that he didn't ask for the job. God called him and there he was. He had nothing to commend himself except God's calling. That's it. Amos had every reason to feel inferior . . . but he didn't.

Now admittedly, I've pressed my point to the extreme, but the lesson is obvious. When your eyes are on yourself, you will not get out of your own home in the morning successfully. The task is too difficult. If your eyes are fixed on the Lord, you can step into life and keep that heart with the Lord, just like Amos did. Whatever the task, you can do it.

A Scriptural Viewpoint

But it isn't just that. Let's get some other things straight. We need to know about *God's* estimate of *us.* Consider some New Testament principles as to what God thinks of you, child of God.

In Matthew 6:26 we hear Jesus' insights.

> "Look at the birds of the air, that they do not sow, neither do they reap, nor gather into barns, and yet your heavenly Father feeds them. Are you not worth much more than they?"

You're worth much to God—that's the point. Jesus is teaching about worry in this passage, but there are other truths here too. If God cares for and sustains a little sparrow in the sky, aren't you worth much more than that small, fragile bird?

> "And which of you by being anxious can add a single cubit to his life's span? [The answer is, "None."] And why are you anxious about clothing? Observe how the lilies of the field grow; they do not toil nor do they spin, yet I say to you that even Solomon in all his glory did not clothe himself like one of these. [And now the climax.] But if God so arrays the grass of the field, which is alive today and tomorrow is thrown into the furnace, will He not much more do so for you, O men of little faith?" (Matt. 6:27–30)

What's He saying? You're worth much more than grass or lilies or sparrows. You are of *infinite* worth to God. You're worth so much to God that He sent His Son to die for you. The next time you begin to think how unworthy and wormy and inferior you feel, remember that to God you are the object of His attention and His affection. If it hadn't been for your sins and mine, there would never have been the need for a Savior. God so *loved* you that He sent His Son. He even seeks your worship (John 4:23); He enjoys being with His children.

Let's look at another way God sees us. In Ephesians 2:10 we learn that we are God's workmanship.

> For we are His workmanship, created in Christ Jesus for good works, which God prepared beforehand, that we should walk in them.

God gives His attention to us as individuals. No two of us are alike. He doesn't look upon the mass of humanity and pick out a glob within that larger mass and say, "Now I'll just shower blessings on the whole group and smear it all over them like peanut butter." He knows each one of us *personally,* and He is working with *each* one—with YOU. I smile as I write that thought.

And Philippians 1:6 says He is not through working with us yet.

> For I am confident of this very thing, that He who began
> a good work in you will perfect it until the day of Christ Jesus.

He who began ... will perfect. The idea is "to complete." He is not through. You are an unfinished project of the living Lord. Think of it!

You may have seen those confusing buttons some people used to wear. They read, "PBPGINFWMY"—"Please be patient ... God is not finished with me yet." That's true! Philippians 1:6 says He will complete the job, but He is not finished yet.

A person who is absorbed with his own inferior feelings

thinks he is not as good as_____, and then he mentally rattles off the names of a number of other people, most of whom he probably can't stand anyway! He forgets that he, personally, is being worked on by God. Our eyes continually scan the surface, comparing ourselves with others. Yet God deals with us individually. He's not finished.

Then Philippians 2:13:

> For it is God who is at work in you, both to will and to work for His good pleasure.

There's a lot of theology in that statement, but let's not get bogged down. It is the first part of the verse that intrigues me: "God is at work in you."

Let's take a long look at the Word of God before we consider our own estimate of ourselves. You are, before the Lord, a very important person. This is not just good psychology; this is good, sound, biblical doctrine. God sent His Son because He loves you. Romans 8:29 says that God is conforming us, since He is working on us as His unique vessels.

Since He is not finished with us, how about considering you and the Lord a team? Rather than competing with someone else, think of yourself and the Lord Jesus Christ in a cooperative relationship. And rather than running against His working, *cooperate* with His workings. He is at work.

Picture yourself as a priceless diamond in the rough. God works away on you, buffeting and polishing, grinding and filing. The diamond is being shaped and prepared for the perfect plan He has for you. But at times the process is definitely irritating. *The one who frequently feels inferior is the one who concentrates on the part that isn't finished rather than on the part that is being completed or has already been shaped.* God is working on you—He just isn't finished. Remember the key word: *persevere!*

Beauty in the Body

The body of Christ is the entire family of God on earth today, all around the world. Every born-again believer in Christ is a member of that universal body. Christ is the head, and some of us are arms, fingers, toes, or parts of the body organs. Some are seen and some are unseen, but all of us together make up one great body. And there's beauty in that arrangement.

Now, with all that in mind, try to read 1 Corinthians 12:14–17 and still feel inferior!

> For the body is not one member, but many. If the foot should say, "Because I am not a hand, I am not a part of the body," it is not for this reason any the less a part of the body. And if the ear should say, "Because I am not an eye, I am not a part of the body," it is not for this reason any the less a part of the body. If the whole body were an eye, where would the hearing be? If the whole were hearing, where would the sense of smell be?

Picture one big ear, six-foot-two! Isn't that gross? Just think of that. Or one big eye. Where would the beauty be? Where would the whole picture be? It would be gone.

Usefulness in the Body

Now look at 1 Corinthians 12:18: "But now God has placed the members, each one of them, in the body, just as He desired."

That's important. He made you a finger because He wants you to be a finger. He made you an arm because He wants you to be an arm. He made you a toe or a foot tucked into a shoe, never seen, because He wants you to be a toe or a foot never seen. It pleases Him! The person who suffers from inferiority suffers because he, a toe, is not an eye. Or because he, a foot, isn't as pretty as a face or a mouth. It conveys the idea that, "Oh, because I'm not this, I'm not useful."

To the *body*, every part is useful.

> And the eye cannot say to the hand, "I have no need of you;" or again the head to the feet, "I have no need of you."
> (1 Cor. 12:21)

Some organs of the body that seem weak may be very important. If some of the organs you never see were not there—my, how the body would suffer! Some of you readers in the family of God are made to be unseen, yet vital, organs. The vital organs *are* the unseen ones, by the way. Stop and think about that. Hidden away behind a stretching of skin and bones and muscles are those vital, unseen organs. When you begin to feel, "I am not as useful as (and you name that person)," remember that the body's vital organs are not really the ones that are seen.

Why does God design the church this way?

> That there should be no division in the body, but that the members should have the same care for one another.
> (1 Cor. 12:25)

One characteristic of the body is that it cares for itself. You can never say, "My finger hurts, but I feel good everywhere else." *That's not normal.* When one member of Christ hurts, the others should hurt. That's normal. If one hurts and the rest of us just roll right on, unconcerned, some sort of alienation has taken place.

The apostle Paul said:

> For through the grace given to me I say to every man among you not to think more highly of himself than he ought to think [don't be conceited]; but to think so as to have sound judgment, as God has allotted to each a measure of faith. (Rom. 12:3)

The *Living Letters* renders this verse:

> As God's messenger I give each of you God's warning: be honest in your estimate of yourselves, measuring your value by how much faith God has given you.

It is of great importance that you have an estimate of yourself that is *honest.*

A Prescription

Now I'm going to prescribe four "Rs." I don't usually do this sort of ditty, but I think it will help you remember some principles.

Having said all that I have about Moses and Jeremiah and Amos, and these passages from the New Testament, there are four suggestions with which I close this chapter. Each one will help you when you're swamped with feelings of inferiority.

The first "R" is *realize* that you were prescribed before birth. Look at Psalm 139:13–16:

> For Thou didst form my inward parts;
> Thou didst weave me in my mother's womb.
> I will give thanks to Thee, for I am fearfully and
>   wonderfully made;
> Wonderful are Thy works,
> And my soul knows it very well.
> My frame was not hidden from Thee,
> When I was made in secret,
> And skillfully wrought in the depths of the earth.
> Thine eyes have seen my unformed substance;
> And in Thy book they were all written,
> The days that were ordained for me,
> When as yet there was not one of them.

We were all prescription babies, every one of us. God made you just like you ought to be—the present color (or quantity) of your hair, notwithstanding. He made you with the face He wants you to have. If He made you seven-feet-one, He wants you seven-feet-one. If He made you four-feet-two. He wants you four-feet-two.

The second "R" is *remember*—the process is still going on. He's not finished. Work hard not to forget that fact.

The third "R" is *refuse* to compare yourself with others. That's going to be the toughest of the four "Rs." If you want to conquer this inferiority, stop looking at those around you and start looking at the Lord. Comparison demoralizes—refuse to do it.

The fourth "R" is *respond* correctly to your weak points. Respond correctly to those things you feel are defects or scars or shortcomings. Try to change them if you can. If you can't, pray very much about them—just as Paul did. View that scar or defect not as a cross to endure but as a unique marking of God on your life.

In summary,

1. *Realize* that you were prescribed before birth.
2. *Remember* that the growth process is still going on.
3. *Refuse* to compare yourself with others.
4. *Respond* correctly to your shortcomings.

A friend of mine, who graduated from the same seminary I graduated from, has a bright red scar, a birthmark, across the side of his face. It's like a burn scar. It stretches in an unattractive, obvious fashion down his forehead and across his nose and down across a large section of his mouth and neck.

As far as I could tell, this man had absolutely no difficulty with inferiority. This is, to say the least, unusual.

One day I worked up the courage to ask him how it was that he could be so effective on his feet and trust God to use him without apparent concern about his looks.

"Because of my dad," he said. "My dad taught me, as far back as I can remember, that this part of my face was where an angel must have kissed me before I was ever born. He said to me, 'Son, this marking was for Dad, so that I might know that you are mine. You have been marked out by God just to remind me that you're my son.'

"All through my young days, as I grew up, I was reminded by my dad, 'You are the most important, special fellow on earth.'

"To tell you the truth," he told me, "I got to where I felt sorry for people who *didn't* have birthmarks across the sides of their faces!"

Until we can thank God for our shortcomings, for the scars in our lives, we will never conquer the problem of inferiority. Why not confess your struggles with inferiority feelings to the Lord right now, before you read further. Ask him to deliver you from your preoccupation with yourself, your constant secret analyzing of how high or low you might be on the "gifts spectrum," and to give you a fresh touch of His Holy Spirit to allow you to feel about yourself the way God feels and cares about you.

It really boils down to what you choose to think about yourself. No one can make you feel inferior without your consent. Only you can ultimately stop the plague of self-doubt.

Only you.

10
Fear: Fierce Grip of Panic

A young woman in our church in California (I'll call her Susan) had an incredible experience late in the winter of 1976. She was a bride of several months, happily anticipating each new dawn. On one particular morning, happiness did not await her.

A knock came at her apartment door. Because her husband had already left for work, Susan was a little uneasy about opening the door. But she did. Standing in front of her was a man she'd never seen before. He seemed nervous, and that increased her uneasiness. He inquired about the location of the manager's apartment. She quickly gave him the information he needed and shut the door.

In only a few minutes, another knock came. Wary, but not enough to restrain her action, Susan opened the door again. The long blade of the same man's knife pushed her back into the room. He locked and bolted the door, closed the drapes, and told her to take off all her clothes.

At that fearful moment, Susan (an outstanding Christian woman) looked into the face of the would-be rapist and, with remarkable calmness, said: "I am a Christian. The Lord Jesus Christ is watching over me right now, and He is not going to allow anything to happen to me He doesn't want to occur."

The man stared at her blankly. He was absolutely dumbfounded.

She continued: "Jesus Christ loves you. He wants to come into your life and become your Lord and Savior." Then she asked rather pointedly, "Have you ever had the gospel explained to you in a way you could understand it?"

He lowered the blade and replied simply, "No."

"Then, please, sit down."

He shoved the knife into his pocket and sank into a chair. For the next hour and a half, Susan and the stranger discussed the claims of Christ. She learned he was new in the area and had no friends, no money, and no purpose in life. He told her an "inner voice" told him to do what he had done that morning.

The courageous woman fearlessly pressed the issue. "Just as I opened my door to you, not knowing fully what to expect on the other side, so you must do the same in your life. Jesus awaits your decision to let Him in. Can you think of any reason you shouldn't do that?"

He couldn't.

She asked him to bow his head, and in his own words to accept the gift God was offering him—His own dear Son.

He did. Shortly thereafter he was gone, never to return. And he never laid a hand on her!

After the man left, Susan was suddenly seized by fierce panic. She was immediately overwhelmed with her narrow escape from danger. Never before had Susan experienced so vividly the truth of Psalm 34.

> I sought the LORD, and He answered me,
> And delivered me from all my fears. . . .
> This poor man cried and the LORD heard him,
> And saved him out of all his troubles.
> The angel of the LORD encamps around those who fear Him,
> And rescues them.
> O taste and see that the LORD is good;

How blessed is the man who takes refuge in Him!
(Ps. 34:4, 6–8)

Susan never heard from the stranger again. But the experience has left an indelible impression on all our minds; God can handle our fears!

Understanding Fear

Wayne W. Dyer has written a best-seller called *Your Erroneous Zones.* Maybe you've read it. In the book he talks about the days when we lose the battle because we are not living in the present moment. We feel guilty about something that happened yesterday or we are afraid about something that might happen tomorrow, and we fail to reach total fulfillment today. Fear can keep us from enjoying *today.* [1]

I know a young collegian who had a summer job as a welder's assistant, building a hospital. He had never welded before in his life. He was afraid of heights, and wouldn't you know, they put him to work welding on the seventeenth floor! Vast sections of steel beams were jutting out over nowhere. He worked, almost immobilized by fear from day to day. Finally, an "incredible hunk" of a welder with whom he was working looked at him and said, "What's the matter, son? Are you scared?"

My friend said, "S-s-scared? I've b-b-been t-t-trying to t-t-tell you for t-t-two weeks 'I q-q-quit!' but I c-c-couldn't get it out of m-m-my m-m-mouth!" He was scared to death. And so are some of you who read these words. Fear immobilizes. It also intimidates.

Overcoming Intimidation

I find a great deal of comfort in what David wrote when he addressed this whole subject of fear:

> The LORD is my light and my salvation;
> Whom shall I fear?
> The LORD is the defense of my life;
> Whom shall I dread? (Ps. 27:1)

Please observe that David did not say the Lord *gives* light or the Lord *provides* strength. He said the Lord *is* light and He *is* strength. That is very important.

We have the Lord inside us, so it makes no difference whether it is a Sunday or a Tuesday or a Saturday morning or a Thursday afternoon; He *is* all these things. And we don't have to be inside a church building to have them. Because the Lord *is* at all times light, defense, and protection, He takes care of those things that bother me.

Look at David's questions. "Whom shall I fear?" That's the normal, everyday word for *fear* in the Hebrew, but the next one is not. "Whom shall I *dread?*" That's the word we're interested in. It means "to be in awe," "to be in dread of someone," or "to be *intimidated.*"

I was in my study early one morning. My wife, Cynthia, called me and said, "Honey, there's a fellow trying to get hold of you. He really sounds depressed. He's from another state—long distance—why don't you call him?" She gave me his number.

I picked up the phone, dialed the operator, gave her my name and his number. He answered the phone with, "Yeah, I'll take the call."

"Swindoll?" he asked.

"Yes," I answered.

He said, "I'm six-foot-six and I weigh over four hundred pounds." A little shiver went down my spine.

And I replied, "Yes sir! What can I do for you, sir?"

He said, "I just heard you on your radio program *Insight for Living*. You are the guy on the radio, aren't you?"

"What area are you in?" I asked. He told me, and I confirmed that I was the one.

He said, "I run twelve service stations and I've fought my way through life for the past thirty years. I've been in and out of church, mostly out. There's nobody I can't whip. But down inside my skin I'm scared to death." (I was so relieved to know *that* was his problem.) He continued.

"On the radio you talked about being free. You talked about being free from fear, even the fear of oneself. Down inside of me there's a little boy that's scared half to death. I've worked out a way to handle this—with my fists. But man, I'm scared! Can you give me some insight about this business of freedom? I really need to conquer my fear."

We talked about fifteen or twenty minutes, and when we were ready to hang up, he said, "I've got to go; I've got to take care of my business. Chuck, I love you." (I was also relieved to hear him say that!)

Here was a huge man who was afraid, like the little boy down inside himself. You know what our conversation said to me? It said that even big people are fearful. Size doesn't guarantee confidence. People you look at and think are the epitome of security and self-confidence are often, down inside, little caged-up boys and girls, scared of themselves and afraid to say it.

"Whom shall I dread? Who will intimidate me?" asked David. Little David. Not even a Goliath intimidated David, because he said the battle was the *Lord's*. The God of David is the God of His children today. He says, "*I* am your light, your salvation, your defense." Well, we reason, maybe David didn't really face the kinds of pressures I face. Let's read about them:

> When evildoers came upon me to devour my flesh,
> My adversaries and my enemies, they stumbled and fell.
> Though a host [he's outnumbered] encamp against me,
> My heart will not fear;
> Though war arise against me [he's overwhelmed].
> (Ps. 27:2–3)

David was fighting alone against an army. How about that for odds? Saul's entire army was sent out to get one man. You know what I thought as I read that? I thought, *That is the height of intimidation!*

When David slipped out of a cave and hid behind a rock, he could hear them all around him. I mean, if the Lord wasn't real to him then, He never would be. The conflict was intense: A host had encamped against him, a war had risen against him. I can hardly believe what he says next: "In spite of this I shall be confident" (Ps. 27:3).

Maintaining Confidence

Confidence does not mean "self-confidence." It doesn't mean human cleverness. It doesn't even mean being smarter than other people. It means "to be secure," "to have assurance." The

Lord was David's single *source* of assurance. That's where the rubber of Christianity meets the road. And you want, more than anything else, to be confident. God wants that for you, too.

Well, how did confidence come to David? He had one thing on his heart:

> One thing I have asked from the LORD, that I shall seek:
> That I may dwell in the house of the LORD all the days of my
>   life,
> To behold the beauty of the LORD,
> And to meditate in His temple. (Ps.27:4)

Don't ask God for a hundred things. Ask for one thing "that I shall seek." Well, what is it, David? Tell me, fast. "That I may dwell in the house of the Lord all the days of my life."

What? You mean I've got to live in a church building? You know that that's not what he means, because he's out in the field, running for his life. Look further. "To behold the beauty of the Lord, and to meditate in His temple."

Now, don't miss it: dwelling in the house and meditating in the temple. Read on.

> For in the day of trouble He will conceal me in His tabernacle;
> In the secret place of His tent He will hide me;
> He will lift me up on a rock. (Ps. 27:5)

Dwelling in the house . . . meditating in the temple . . . concealed in the tabernacle . . . hidden in the tent. All that helps replace fear with confidence. That sounds so good to me. But what does he mean in all this?

In David's day, the imagery of the psalms was such that being "in a dwelling place" meant being surrounded by protection. In our terms it would mean conscious, continuous fellowship with the living Lord in the midst of His people. One man has called it "practicing the presence of God."

David was saying, "When I walk out of this cave, not knowing where the spears are coming from, I know that in the tent, in the tabernacle, in the house, in the temple, surrounded by Your protection, I am safe. That's one thing I ask, Lord— that nothing break our relationship."

When we are intimidated, when we lack confidence, we are invariably more conscious of the person attacking us than we are of the Lord. When we step into a scene that is intimidating to us, we must consciously see ourselves in the tent, meditating in the tabernacle, beholding the beauty of the Lord and saying to Him, "Right now, God, I don't have anything I can draw upon; I'm all Yours."

At this point, David began to pray:

Hear, O LORD, when I cry with my voice,
And be gracious to me and answer me [it's an imperative,
   like a command].
When Thou didst say, "Seek My face," my heart said to Thee,
"Thy face, O LORD, I shall seek."
Do not hide Thy face from me,
Do not turn Thy servant away in anger;
Thou hast been my help;
Do not abandon me nor forsake me,
O God of my salvation! (Ps. 27:7–9)

This is not a halfhearted petition. David meant every word of it. We tend to fiddle around with prayer. God says, "I promise you My presence. Link yourself to Me. Count on Me, and I'll get you through this threatening situation."

And we say something cold and formal, like, "All right, Lord, if perchance You will, please lead, guide, and direct me."

Hey, that's not the kind of prayer God wants!

"Lord, right now! I take you at Your Word. I *cannot* go into this situation without You. I say to You, *answer* me, *provide* my need, *give me the gutsy strength* I need this very moment."

Sometimes in the car, as I'm driving to a situation that will be extremely threatening, not knowing what it will hold for me, I pray out loud. People on the street look at me very strangely. I really don't care too much what they're thinking. They're not going to face that situation—I am!

Staying Balanced

Perhaps you are thinking, "It sounds to me like David (and Swindoll) is getting a little fanatical." I don't think so. Look what he says in Psalm 27:11:

> Teach me Thy way, O LORD,
> And lead me in a level path,
> Because of my foes.

"Teach me, Lord, and lead me in a balanced fashion, because I have a lot of enemies. Keep me balanced. Level me out."

Now look at 27:13. It's so true.

> I would have despaired unless I had believed that
> I would see the goodness of the LORD

In the land of the living [that is, where I'm at right *now*!].

"I could never have walked out to face what I had to face, Lord, without You here with me. Despair would have defeated me. I would have cracked up."

Releasing Fear's Fierce Grip

Sometime ago, Cynthia and I spent a wonderful evening with Ruth Harms Calkin and her husband, Rollin. Ruth has written *Tell Me Again, Lord, I Forget,*² *Lord, You Love to Say Yes,*³ and other excellent works worth reading.

Mrs. Calkin is a godly woman, one I deeply admire. She's learned, literally in a bed of affliction, what it is to trust God. At the age of nineteen she met Rollin, and they planned to be married soon. But she developed a persistent cough, and they found a cavity in her lung which, in those days, could be treated only through an intense period of hospitalization. So she left for a sanitorium, where she was on her back for *two years.*

In all the trauma that accompanied this setback, her love for her fiancé grew. During her stay in the hospital, she began to record her thoughts in prayer. When the average person would have said, "There's no way . . . I despair," she believed. She presented these thoughts to God and kept them in a journal. Finally, she was released from the hospital, and she and Rollin were married. Through a chain of events, they were led into a Christian ministry.

Just about the time they were thinking of beginning their family, Ruth suffered another coughing spell. Clammy fingers of fear began to wrap themselves around her. Tests were made, and a cavity was found on the *other* lung. She faced the possibility of another prolonged hospitalization. The fierce grip of panic began to squeeze her tightly, and she fell apart before God.

After leaving a note for Rollin along with the doctor's report, Ruth took a long walk. Her husband read it and immediately drove out to the place where she was walking—along a railroad track. She was in great despair. He ran to her, and they embraced. "I'm with you no matter what," he told her.

The events that followed were tragic. There was another intense bout with tuberculosis. The doctor suggested they never have children. So they didn't. But they told us that they have ministered with literally hundreds of kids in choir programs and in the ministry of Christian education, as God has used them at the First Baptist Church of Pomona, California.

Today, she ministers as she never could have ministered if it hadn't been for the blows of having to wait, stay quiet, and believe in the goodness of the Lord in the land of the living. She cast away fear. She released its grip as she faced it head-on in God's strong power.

I'm honestly afraid that some of you reading this book will miss the best things God has for you by *running* instead of *trusting* when you are afraid. Here is a practical way for you to handle your fears.

1. As they occur, *admit* them. Say, "I am fearful of (and identify it)." Nothing is ever conquered until it is openly and clearly identified.

2. As you admit them, *commit* them to God. Be very practical here. Spell out your decision to rest your case with Him. Be specific. Verbally declare yourself. Turn that steel grip over to God. Tell Him it's His to handle.

3. As you commit your fears to God, *release* them. God says, "I've heard; I'll take the fear." In another psalm, David said:

Cast your burden upon the LORD, and He will sustain you;
He will never allow the righteous to be shaken. (Ps. 55:22)

4. Stand firm. In God's almighty, invincible strength, consciously *refuse to retreat*. God honors that kind of faith.

Many years ago, my sister Luci, who is two years older than I, was a field representative for the college she graduated from in Texas. Her major responsibility was to acquaint young women with the college and to encourage them to attend—ideally, to recruit them. It was a good job with one serious drawback. She was required to drive many miles alone. As a single woman, she couldn't be too careful.

While on a lengthy recruitment trip one week, she noticed in her rearview mirror that she was being followed by a man alone in his car. Attempts to ditch him proved futile. Since it was about dusk, she was hesitant to press on to the next city. Fear seized her as she imagined being forced over on the side of the road by the stranger.

She decided to pull in at the nearest motel and guarantee a greater measure of security behind a locked door. As she registered, she saw the man about half a block away, waiting. Blinded by panic and sick with fear, she hurriedly carried her things into the small motel room . . . and immediately boltlocked the door and snapped the chain into the slot. Tears of horror filled her eyes as she heard his car pull up outside her room.

She decided right then to admit her vulnerability to God . . . to declare her fear, her panic, her insecure feelings. She forced herself to carry on—she needed a shower and a good night's sleep—but the thought of a possible middle-of-the-night attack robbed her of any semblance of inner peace. What could she do?

Just as she was at the point of emotional distraction, Luci turned and glanced at the top of the dresser. To her amazement, someone had written these words and slipped them under the glass on top:

> Come to Me, all who are weary and heavy laden, and I will give you rest.
>
> Signed: *Jesus*

An incredible surge of strength swept through her. The intimidating dread of an attack was gone. Christ-confidence replaced panic. Assurance of God's presence suddenly became a very present reality as she released herself into His everlasting arms. She told me later that she slept like a baby all night long, and there was not even a hint of trouble. Knowing her, she probably sang herself to sleep.

The fierce grip of panic need not immobilize you. God knows no limitation when it comes to deliverance. Admit your fear. Commit it to Him. Dump the pressure on Him; He can handle it.

Ask Susan. Or Luci. Either one will tell you how marvelous it is to experience freedom from fear.

11

Anger: Burning Fuse of Hostility

A great American statesman, Thomas Jefferson, worked out a way to handle his anger. He included it in his "Rules of Living," which describes how he believed adult men and women should live. He wrote this:

> When angry, count ten before you speak;
> If very angry, a hundred.[1]

Author Mark Twain, about seventy-five years later, revised Jefferson's words. He wrote:

> When angry, count four.
> When very angry, swear.[2]

Those of us with a streak of honesty will have to say we've tried nearly everything from Jefferson's philosophy to Twain's, and we still can't seem to handle our anger very effectively. It's a real problem. If you wrestle with a bad temper, you may be laughing on the outside, but crying on the inside. I don't know of anything more frustrating to deal with than anger (it makes me mad!). It has a way of disarming us, of robbing us of our testimonies. It injures our home lives and our relationships with coworkers.

Sometime ago a man sat in my study and poured out his anguish. He had battered his wife the night before. She was too humiliated (and bruised) to come with him. Both, by the way, are Christians.

I sat in the Orange County jail with a young father, his face buried in his hands. Tears ran through his fingers as he told me of his temper. He had just killed his infant daughter with his own hands—in an uncontrollable rage. He had been irritated by the baby's crying as he was listening to music.

No, anger isn't a humorous matter. It's something that must be understood, admitted, and kept under control, or it will literally slay us.

What Is Anger?

Let me begin by defining what anger is, and that's not easy. I've woven together several different resources and have come up with this definition:

> Anger is an emotional reaction of hostility that brings personal displeasure, either to ourselves or to someone else.

People who study psychology tell us there are various phases of anger. All of us have experienced some of them.

Anger can begin with *mild irritation,* which is nothing more than perhaps an innocent experience of being upset, a mild feeling of discomfort brought about by someone or something.

Then anger can turn from irritation to *indignation,* which is a feeling that something must be answered; there must be an avenging of that which is wrong. But both irritation and indignation can go unexpressed.

If fed, indignation leads to *wrath—*which *never* goes

unexpressed. Psychologists tell us that wrath is a strong desire to avenge.

Then, as it increases, anger becomes *fury.* The word suggests violence, even a loss of emotional control.

The last phase of anger is *rage.* Obviously, rage is the most dangerous form of anger.

In Los Angeles sometime back, a man drowned his children—four of them. He admitted it happened in a fit of rage. Rage is a temporary loss of control involving acts of violence; the angry person scarcely realizes what he has done.

The Scriptures May Surprise You!

In Ephesians 4:26–27 we have two verses that have to do with anger.

> Be angry, and yet do not sin; do not let the sun go down on your anger, and do not give the devil an opportunity.

The Amplified Bible renders those verses this way:

> When angry, do not sin; do not ever let your wrath—your exasperation, your fury or indignation—last until the sun goes down. Leave no [such] room or foothold for the devil—give no opportunity to him.

The New English Bible says it this way:

> If you are angry, do not let anger lead you into sin; do not let sunset find you still nursing it; leave no loop-hole for the devil.

The very first time I looked at this verse in depth, I did a double-take. Do you realize that God is saying to you, "Get mad!" That's right. If that were the end of verse 26, we would put an exclamation point after the word *angry*. Be angry! How about that! When's the last time you obeyed the Scriptures and "blew your cool"?

I see three important things in these verses. The first is simple and clear. *Anger is a God-given emotion.* There's something inhuman about a person who never gets angry. He has a strange makeup. We would be quick to say that one who does not show compassion really does not have a heart. And one who doesn't love—well, there's something terribly wrong with him. These emotions are God-given, and He says to express them. The same is true of anger. God says, "Be angry."

The second observation goes right along with the first. *Anger is not necessarily sinful.* God says, "Be angry, and yet do not sin." Not every expression of anger is wrong. It's as though I were to say to one of my children, "Now, when you go out tonight, enjoy yourself. Really have a good time. But don't misuse your humor." Or it's like the Lord when He says, "I want you to love, but don't love the world. Don't even love the things of the world. I want you to love, but restrict that love to certain things." This is the same thought. Be angry, but don't carry that anger to the point where it becomes sin.

Some of you may be questioning whether or not it is *ever* right to be angry. Did you know that in the Old Testament "the anger of the Lord" is mentioned no less than eighteen times?

And in the New Testament we have some classic examples of Jesus' anger! When those moneychangers were in the temple, He didn't walk in and say, "Now listen, guys, I don't want to offend you, but what you are doing isn't very good." Rather, he plaited together a whip of thongs and physically drove them out of the temple. His was an expression of real indignation. He got mad!

And Jesus never spoke more angrily and forthrightly to anyone than He did to the religious hypocrites in Matthew 23, where in one case after another He said, "Woe to you." He even called them "whitewashed tombs" and "serpents"! There are times when anger is very appropriate. I'll say more about that later.

Third, *anger must have safeguards.* Notice the two safeguards Paul gave us right in this passage?

Safeguard number one: "Do not let the sun go down on your anger" (Eph. 4:26).

Don't prolong anger into the night. In Paul's day, the setting of the sun was the closing of the day and the beginning of the next. By the end of the day, make sure your anger problem is solved.

I believe this is to be taken very literally. We practice this in our home; perhaps you do in yours. If there have been times of disagreement or anger throughout the day, clear them up by evening. When you lay your head on your pillow, make sure those feelings of anger have been resolved. Be certain that there is forgiveness, a clearing out of that conscience. Husbands and wives, don't go to sleep back to back. Don't allow yourself the luxury of feeling you can take care of it later on.

Every once in a while, a Christian brother or sister tells me of an experience when they flew off the handle. They were in the wrong. And they will say something like, "You know, as I turned in that night, things just didn't settle right." Maybe you've had that experience. I certainly have. Then they say, "I had to get up, turn the light on, and make a phone call . . . or get dressed, go over to this person's house, and talk with him face to face to clear it up." It's a real encouragement to hear things like that.

That's what Paul was saying. Don't let sin come in by prolonging your anger. There are probably some scars in your life that are there because you didn't solve anger when it occurred. You know, 99 percent of all problems never solve themselves. Never! They just stay on like a burr in the saddle, until a sore is formed and you become diseased.

Safeguard number two: "Do not give the devil an opportunity" (Eph. 4:27).

That means just what it says. Don't allow your anger to be expressed in such a way that you are weakened and the devil reproduces his character through you.

You see, Jesus Christ loves to reproduce His character through us. When we are under the control of the Holy Spirit, then the character of Christ flows freely—His love, His gentleness, His compassion, His joy, His concern for others. But the devil is a master of counterfeit, and when we are given over to the things of Satan, he aims to make us behave as he does.

That's Paul's whole point. Don't let anger get hold of you and weaken you so that other areas of sin, or even satanic involvement, can come into your life. Keep that in mind if you are prone to get angry. Sustained, uncontrolled anger offers the enemy of our souls an open door. It's serious.

Let's face it: We're all made up differently. Some of us are more emotional than others. Some have much more trouble controlling anger than others. You know how you are made, what your areas of weakness are. And when you sense that it's getting to the point where it's beyond your control, you know the Lord is not in it. Don't give the devil an opportunity.

Anger: Burning Fuse of Hostility

When Is Anger Justified?

When can we actually say it is right to be angry? That's an important question. I find there are three specific situations in Scripture when anger is justifiable.

1. When God's Word and God's will are knowingly disobeyed by God's people
Something should happen in the heart of the child of God who sees other believers sinning openly, ignoring and disobeying the will of God. It's not good for us to look on passively. Something's wrong! When Moses saw what was going on around that golden calf, he couldn't handle it. He got downright indignant (see Exod. 32:19–20).

Further, there is an instance in Solomon's life that shows us the Lord does not overlook acts of carnality. First Kings 11 is the very sad tale of Solomon's last years. He had been blessed with riches, the likes of which the world has never known. The late J. Paul Getty would look like a bum compared to Solomon. He was loaded. And he had more wives and concubines, it seems, than any other man who has ever lived. He had more wisdom than anyone else in Scripture. But look at the latter part of his life.

Now King Solomon loved many foreign women along with the daughter of Pharaoh: Moabite, Ammonite, Edomite, Sidonian, and Hittite women, from the nations concerning which the LORD had said to the sons of Israel, you shall not associate with them, neither shall they associate with you, for they will surely turn your heart away after their gods." Solomon held fast to these in love.

> And he had seven hundred wives, princesses, and three hundred concubines, and his wives turned his heart away. For it came about when Solomon was old, his wives turned his heart away after other gods; and his heart was not wholly devoted to the LORD his God, as the heart of David his father had been. (1 Kings 11:1–4)

The next four verses describe his idolatrous practices. Then we read:

> Now the LORD was angry with Solomon because his heart was turned away from the LORD, the God of Israel, who had appeared to him twice, and had commanded him concerning this thing, that he should not go after other gods; but he did not observe what the LORD had commanded. (1 Kings 11:9–10)

Anger is justified not only on man's part, but on the Lord's part when we openly and knowingly disobey His Word. On some fronts, grace has been twisted to convey the idea that God no longer has any standards, or that a godly quality of life is not expected of us, now that we're under grace. That is a perversion and a lie right out of the pit of hell!

The Scriptures show us that the Lord always has and always will become intensely angry when we choose to openly disobey Him. If you are continuing to live in open, knowing disobedience to God, I warn you that the Lord's anger is kindled against you. (I will deal with this at length in my next chapter on defection.) By His grace, He might permit you the time to see this, but I assure you that it will bear tremendous consequences.

There are other occasions in the Bible in which anger is justified.

2. When God's enemies assume positions of jurisdiction outside their rights
The prophet Isaiah records an example of the Lord's enemies moving into a realm outside their rights. The Lord rebuked them for it.

> Woe to those who call evil good, and good evil;
> Who substitute darkness for light and light for darkness. . . .
> Woe to those who are wise in their own eyes,
> And clever in their own sight!
> Woe to those who are heroes in drinking wine,
> And valiant men in mixing strong drink;
> Who justify the wicked for a bribe [and now here's the
>   phrase],
> And take away the rights of the ones
>   who are in the right! [Woe to them!] . . .
> Therefore, as a tongue of fire consumes stubble . . .
> So their root will become like rot and their blossom blow
>   away as dust;
> For they have rejected the law of the LORD of hosts,
> And despised the word of the Holy One of Israel.
> On this account the anger of the LORD has burned against
> His people. (Isa. 5:20–25)

The little phrase in verse 23 attracts my attention. "Those who take away the rights of the ones who are in the right!" My point is this: Anger is justified when enemies of the Lord take away rights outside their realm of jurisdiction. Several examples could be shown from Scripture.

For example, in 1 Samuel 11 Saul is the anointed king when an enemy comes to invade the land. We read in 1 Samuel 11:6 that "the Spirit of God came upon Saul mightily when he heard these words, and he became very angry." Literally, his anger became intense, because war was being declared against the land of God and the people of Israel. Their freedom was being threatened.

I think this is very applicable for our day and our view of war. I can assure you that I am not a warmonger. No one hurts more than I do to see the results of war. No doubt, you feel the same. But this is not to say that when an enemy desires to come in and remove the freedom of our land that we should sit passively by and say, "Well, we just had better live with it. It's just one of those problems of life. Evil is on the earth." The Scriptures declare that when people take away the rights of those who are in the right, the Lord becomes *angry* . . . and so should we. Defending these treasured rights is our responsibility.

3. When children are dealt with unfairly by parents.
Here in Ephesians 6 we are no longer dealing with theory or some distant war or some court of law. We are now talking about justified anger in the home. I want to be very careful how I express myself, so that I won't be misunderstood.

Children, obey your parents in the Lord, for this is right. Honor your father and mother (which is the first commandment with a promise), that it may be well with you, and that you may live long on the earth. And, fathers, do not provoke your children to anger; but bring them up in the discipline and instruction of the Lord. (Eph. 6:1–4)

The parallel verse in Colossians is, "Fathers, do not exasperate your children, that they may not lose heart" (Col. 3:21).

It is interesting that in both passages, the apostle Paul specifically addressed *fathers*. We fathers often are given to impatience; to a lack of real understanding of the feelings of our little ones, our teenagers, or our young adults still living at home. When we exasperate our children by dealing with them unfairly and they respond in anger, this anger is justified. Do not provoke your children to anger!

And children, be careful that you do not look upon every word from your father's lips as provoking you to anger. I'm talking about those things fathers do that really bring about feelings of unfair hurt and irritation.

We dads get in a hurry. We don't want to take the time to consider people's feelings, so we make demands and say foolish things that are unfair and uncalled for. I confess, my own words convict me!

A perfect illustration of this tension would be the Bible's report on Jonathan. Saul said to his son Jonathan, "Where's David?" And Jonathan said, "He isn't here; he's gone." Saul began to rebuke Jonathan. In fact, the words that are used in the original text suggest the idea of perversion. If I read the Hebrew correctly, Saul makes an accusation suggesting that his son and David are involved in illicit sexual activity. Unfair!

Jonathan became indignant with his father. He said, "What has David done? What wrong has he done?" And then, after his father threw a spear at him to kill him, Jonathan stood, rebuked his father in anger, and left a perfect illustration of what can happen when a father provokes his child to anger.

I want to say something that might be misunderstood, but I am still going to say it. I think some of us are twisting the teaching of the "chain of command" in the home way beyond its proper bounds. Anyone can take a good truth and pervert it, and I know of cases where this has been done.

Be careful as a husband, a father, a man of God, that your dealings with your family are *fair* and that you can, before God, support them scripturally and logically. Be sensitive to your wife and children. Don't use the concept of the chain of command as a brutal, bloody club, lording it over your family. Instead, be an authority that *serves*.[3]

Are you given to unjustified anger? Have doors been slammed closed in your home or with your friends simply because you lost your temper? Ephesians 4:31–32 reads:

> Let all bitterness and wrath and anger and clamor and slander be put away from you, along with all malice. And be kind to one another, tender-hearted, forgiving each other, just as God in Christ also has forgiven you.

Be willing to lay this problem of a short fuse before the Lord. Perhaps a mild irritation leads you to be impatient, and before you know it everything blows. Your testimony is at stake.

The wrath of God was poured out on Jesus Christ at Calvary. All his anger at sin was, at that point in time, poured out on the Savior. He knows what anger is like; you can pour yours out upon Him. He wants to take that weakness, that area of sin, and give you victory in it.

Unjustified Anger

Let's dig deeper. We can't leave the subject until we look at the other side of the coin. When is anger unjustified?

1. When anger comes from the wrong motive
We've all studied the prodigal son, but we usually miss the prodigal that stayed home! He is the one who illustrates an anger that was not justified because it sprang from a wrong motive. When the younger brother came to himself, he was, you will recall, in a swine pen. He was at the end of his rope, and the Scripture says:

> But when he came to his senses, he said, ". . . I will get up and go to my father, and will say to him, 'I am no longer worthy to be called your son; make me as one of your hired men.'" (Luke 15:17–19)

And he did that. You know the rest of the story. The father greeted him with open arms, delighted to have him there. But this joy was not shared by the wayward son's older brother.

> Now his older son was in the field, and when he came and approached the house, he heard music and dancing. And he summoned one of the servants and began inquiring what these things might be. And he said to him, "Your brother has come, and your father has killed the fattened calf, because he has received him back safe and sound." (Luke 15:25–27)

Now notice the *jealous motive* that resulted in anger.

> But he became angry, and was not willing to go in; and his father came out and began entreating him. But he answered and said to his father, "Look! For so many years I have been serving you, and I have never neglected a command of yours; and yet you have never given me a kid, that I might be merry with my friends; But when this son of yours came [notice he doesn't call him "my brother;" he was tremendously angry], who has devoured your wealth with harlots [How does he know that? The Bible never tells us his brother visited prostitutes. It's possible, but when you're angry and jealous, you exaggerate the story.], you killed the fattened calf for him."
>
> And he [the father] said to him, "My child, you have always been with me, and all that is mine is yours. But we had to be merry and rejoice, for this brother of yours was dead and has begun to live, and was lost and has been found." (Luke 15:28–32)

When we are jealous of some other person, our response is frequently one of anger, especially when that other person receives some kind of commendation or promotion or attention from other people. "It isn't fair! That's my right to enjoy, not his!" That anger is unjustified.

Another case in point would be King Nebuchadnezzar. His anger was kindled by the motive of pride. That really does hit us in the heart, because we all wrestle with that old pride problem. Nebuchadnezzar had an immense golden image built— possibly an image of himself. He put it out in a public place and announced that everyone was to worship the image. It was idolatry in the grossest sense of the word. Nebuchadnezzar, filled with pride, announced through his heralds that everyone should worship this image—in other words, that they should worship Nebuchadnezzar.

It just so happened that some chose not to worship the image.

> There are certain Jews whom you have appointed over the administration of the province of Babylon, namely Shadrach, Meshach, and Abed-nego. These men, O king, have disregarded you; they do not serve your gods or worship the golden image which you have set up. (Dan. 3:12)

As a result, something happened in Nebuchadnezzar's heart. Notice the response:

> Then Nebuchadnezzar in rage and anger [Why? Pride.] gave orders to bring Shadrach, Meshach, and Abed-nego; then these men were brought before the king. (Dan. 3:13)

This led to the fiery furnace and to God's miraculous deliverance of these Jewish believers from danger and death.

The thing we must ask ourselves when anger begins to come is, "What is the motive behind my feelings?"

2. When things don't go your way
The Book of Jonah contains the most extensive revival recorded in history. The entire city of Nineveh—believed by many Old Testament scholars to be half a million or more in population—repented of their sins and turned to the Lord.

Jonah, of course, was a bigoted racist. He was a prophet, indeed, but he was a man who really wanted to see Nineveh destroyed, something of an ancient Archie Bunker! That is why he didn't go to Nineveh when God told him to the first time. He did not want Nineveh to repent; he wanted it blasted away. And he got angry because things didn't go his way.

> When God saw their deeds, that they turned from their wicked way, then God relented concerning the calamity which He had declared He would bring upon them. And He did not do it. But it greatly displeased Jonah, and he became angry. (Jon. 3:10–4:1)

Notice that the reason for his anger was that he didn't get his way—he wanted destruction, but God gave deliverance.

> And he prayed to the LORD and said, "Please, LORD, was not this what I said while I was still in my own country? ["This is why I didn't want to go in the first place."] . . . Therefore now, O LORD, please take my life from me, for death is better to me than life."
> And the LORD said, "Do you have good reason to be angry?" (Jon. 4:2–4)

Jonah went out to a hillside, refusing to answer the Lord. He sat down under a nice, leafy gourd vine to enjoy a little shade. Sitting comfortably there on that hill, the wind blowing softly, he thought, *My, this is living.* Here, he could quickly forget about Nineveh. Then a little worm came and ate up that gourd plant, and it wilted. Jonah got hot and bothered, and begged God to take his life. "Then God said to Jonah, 'Do you have good reason to be angry about the plant'?" (Jonah 4:9).

This brings us to a very practical point: We really do like to have our own way. For example, you work hard all week and you think, *I will have a nice evening out with my wife on Friday night.* You get it all arranged, and you drive to your favorite restaurant. There's a long line, but you are not worried. You walk up to the front and say, "I called in reservations for tonight."

The hostess says, "I'm sorry, sir, but I don't have your name written down here."

How do you respond? Unless I miss my guess, you become angry. Rather than saying, "Lord, what can I learn through this?" you think, *Listen, I've got my rights!*

"But I called in two days ago," you protest.

"Sorry."

So you wait in line. Steaming. Frowning. When you finally are seated, you get a bad table (it's near the door or the legs are uneven) and your waitress is irritable. Your food is cold. The candle goes out. The people around you are loud and boisterous.

This is where Christianity is put on the block. The real test is not in a Sunday service. It's in a Friday night restaurant when things don't go our way.

One of the best ways I know to keep from getting angry when we don't get our way is to have a good sense of humor. Turn the bad times into a little fun.

When we were living in Texas, our family planned for months to go to a state park for a camping vacation. We looked forward to it, but before we left we prayed, "Lord, whatever happens, we're going to have a good time."

It was a good thing we prayed that, because the place was a rathole. There were wall-to-wall people. It was hot—the weather was terrible! It was a great disappointment. We spent one night with spiders and scorpions, laughed it off, and headed back home. On the way, we stopped off at another state park where there wasn't a soul. I still can't understand it. We checked in and spent almost two full weeks in a place that was marvelously quiet and delightful, unseasonably cool and picturesque.

God seems to reward us with good, delightful experiences when we move with joy through those times when we didn't get our own way. The choice is ours. If we choose to be offended when we don't get our own way, then we're going to live constantly on the edge of anger. But if we say to ourselves, "A merry heart does good like a medicine," it'll make all the difference in the world.

3. *When you react too quickly without investigating the facts.*

The end of a matter is better than its beginning; Patience of spirit is better than haughtiness of spirit. Do not be eager in your heart to be angry, for anger resides in the bosom of fools. (Eccl. 7:8–9).

But let everyone be quick to hear, slow to speak and slow to anger (James 1:19).

If we have a *patient* spirit, if we *hear a matter out,* it is better than just hearing its beginning. If we are eager in our hearts to be angry, we're foolish.

It's a real concern to me that we have to live at such a hurried, harried pace. When the schedule is not met, the instant response of the foolish one is anger. Retaliate. Fight back. The writer of Ecclesiastes is saying, "If you do that, you're a fool."

This struck me during one of our family vacations. It was amazing how much more patient we were when we got some times of sustained quietness. We were camping deep in the heart of the giant redwoods up near the Oregon border. Beneath the glow of our little red Coleman lantern, we sat around a fire each night. Quietness was all around. Each morning we arose to the chirp of birds and the river's rippling rapids. I don't think we'll ever forget it! As I recall, we didn't have one bout with anger during the whole three weeks.

Develop the art of quietness. Turn off the appliances, including the TV. In fact, wean yourself from it for an entire evening. Leave it off. Honestly, we will never become men and women of God without experiencing some solitude.

This is where the greats of the past had it over us. Men and women who walked with God did so because of their depth of life cultivated in silence. Part of the reason, fathers, that we are so irritable in our homes is that we're keeping such a rapid pace. "He who is slow to anger is better than the mighty, and he who rules his spirit, than he who captures a city" (Prov. 16:32).

Winning Over Anger

What do we do about anger? *When it comes from a wrong motive, when we don't get our own way, when we act in haste—* anger is sin. What practical things does God say about dealing with anger? Scripture offers four specific directives in the book of Proverbs. Let's cover them quickly.

1. Learn to ignore petty disagreements.

A man's discretion makes him slow to anger,
And it is his glory to overlook a transgression. (Prov. 19:11)

Perhaps it is better rendered in the Berkeley Version. "It is prudent for a man to restrain his anger; it is his glory to overlook an offense (MLB).

In God's eyes, it is *glory* if you are big enough to overlook an offense. Don't look for a fight, Christian. Keep the chip off your shoulder. Don't be defensive about your point or your right. Be willing to give.

Proverbs 17:14 says essentially the same thing. I like this verse. "The beginning of strife is like letting out water, so abandon the quarrel before it breaks out."

Just as in the tango, it takes two to quarrel. If you see that there is an angry disagreement coming, back off; leave it. Learn to ignore petty differences.

2. Refrain from close association with anger-prone people. Don't hang around them.

> Do not associate with a man given to anger;
> Or go with a hot-tempered man,
> Lest you learn his ways,
> And find a snare for yourself. (Prov. 22:24–25)

It's true: We become like those we spend our time with. If you spend time with a rebel you will become rebellious and angry. If I hang around people who are negative, you know what happens to me? I become negative. (And by nature, I'm a positive person.) But it's amazing—the more I'm around people who talk about how things won't work, and how this isn't good, and how even though there were ten very fine things, two things went wrong, the more I begin to think, *You know, a lot of things are wrong.* Then I get petty and negative in other areas.

176

Are you becoming an angry person because you're associating closely with angry people? The Scripture says, "Don't do it!"

3. Keep very close check on your tongue.
More than any slanderous event, any immoral act, any unwise financial dealings, that which breaks up a church quickest is an unchecked tongue. The longer I live, the more I realize that.

> A gentle answer turns away wrath,
> But a harsh word stirs up anger. (Prov. 15:1)

> He who guards his mouth and his tongue,
> Guards his soul from troubles. (Prov. 21:23)

Washington Irving made this statement: "The only edged tool that gets sharper with use is the tongue."[4]

It isn't your leg muscle that's the strongest muscle in your body; it's the muscle in your mouth. Control your tongue. It will literally "turn away wrath."

4. Cultivate honesty in communication . . . don't let anger build up.
Take a close look at Proverbs 27:4–6:

> Wrath is fierce and anger is a flood,
> But who can stand before jealousy?
> Better is open rebuke
> Than love that is concealed.
> Faithful are the wounds of a friend,
> But deceitful are the kisses of an enemy.

The New Testament counterpart to this passage is Ephesians 4:25:

Therefore, laying aside falsehood, speak truth, each one of you, with his neighbor, for we are members of one another.

There is no substitute for total honesty, spoken in love. Allowing anger to seethe on the back burner will lead to a very large lid blowing off a very hot pot. Let me encourage you to pick up a copy of David Augsburger's fine book *Caring Enough to Confront.*[5] In that little volume you'll find an excellent treatment of this whole subject. Augsburger offers some outstanding guidelines on how to communicate honestly, yet lovingly.

Well, you've done enough thinking about anger. Enough of theory! Now it's time to put it into action. Not like Mark Twain suggested, or even like Thomas Jefferson . . . but like the Bible directs.

If you begin to implement these inspired principles, you might change your pattern to four steps forward and only one step back!

12
Defection: Final Stage of Compromise

The man who took me under his wing and discipled me for eighteen months when I was overseas in the Marine Corps had been led to Christ by a famous evangelist in a crusade held at Long Beach. Shortly after that campaign, the evangelist who led him to Christ defected from the faith. His family was broken apart. He wandered across the United States like a homeless animal, and finally died a drunkard in a south Chicago gutter.

Another young man with whom my wife and I worked for more than four years was, in our opinion, one of the choicest men we had ever met. God's hand was very firmly placed on his life. He was gifted in an altogether unique way, both academically and in the things of the Lord. He was called into the ministry, and we prayed with him often over a long period of time that God would polish him and prepare him as a chosen vessel for a unique place of service.

Then, through a chain of events, this man began to doubt. Although he was enrolled in seminary and was well able to make the grade, he slowly but surely eroded in his faith. The last time we visited together, he hardly resembled the young man I'd known in years past. He was a cynical shipwreck of the faith, living far from the living Lord. His sentences were punctuated with profuse profanity and caustic comments about Christianity.

Early in my Christian life, I was engaged in the musical side of evangelistic work. I worked with many young men who 'preached the gospel very faithfully and forthrightly. We traveled together through the southwestern United States, engaged in evangelism. God's blessing was very generous to us, and I shall never forget some of the stirring messages these young men brought. Although they had received no seminary training, God was using their lives and their lips.

Today, one of those men is a washout. I talked to his family a few years ago. They were brokenhearted over the fact that he no longer claims the Lord Jesus Christ and no longer lives for Him.

Not all cases of defection are as obvious or notorious as these, and certainly they're not as public. But there's not a church today that's working for Christ and His kingdom that does not experience defection in the lives of some within the assembly.

Frankly, you may be very close to that quitting point yourself. Perhaps you have seriously entertained the thought of going your own way, or you may be presently engaged in a life that is dishonoring to Christ.

Because you rarely find such direct warning in our popular Christian books, I want to talk very straightforwardly with you in this chapter. I want to show you how defection begins, and why you must immediately turn from it. Let me warn you ahead of time that I am going to be direct and perhaps a little blunt.

If you have been joined by faith to the Lord Jesus Christ, you are a child of God. You may deny Him, but He will never deny you; although you are faithless, He will remain faithful. And the grace of God, the seal of the Holy Spirit, preserves you permanently. Salvation is by grace through faith, not of ourselves. We receive it as a gift—by faith, not works. It's a gift that

God gives, and He seals us with His Spirit so we will know Him forever.

But I'll tell you, when you choose to walk away from the Lord and thumb your nose at His grace, He sets the hounds of heaven against you. He does not let His children run wayward or play in the streets of the world without exerting a great deal of discipline. God is very serious about this. You never find a place in the Bible where God no longer calls the people of Israel His children—they're still His, and so are you if you've received Him. But when you're in the divine woodshed and under His discipline, you know it. It's miserable and bitter. Now let's look at some biblical examples of defection.

An Expert on Defection

Centuries ago, there lived a man named Josiah. He had taken over the leadership of the kingdom of Judah when he was eight years old. When he was sixteen he began to seek after the Lord, and he gave himself to Him. At twenty, he overturned all the idols of Baal and Ashteroth. He swept the land clean, and a spiritual awakening came like a fresh, cool breeze in the desert. Josiah had made such an impact that his name was a household word on the lips of the people of Judah. But when he died, after this great revival, the people went right back to the same old sins of days past.

A prophet named Jeremiah spoke for God and wrote strong words in those days—he lived in this transition era. You have heard the expression, "prophet of doom." Jeremiah was in every sense of the word a prophet of doom. He had to be, for he saw where the sins of his people were taking them, and he told them in every way he could, "Death is coming; bondage is ahead; captivity is around the corner. Doom is inevitable if you keep on. So change your mind. Turn around. REPENT!" But they ignored his words. For forty years they ignored him.

Jeremiah lived to see the day of doom, when Babylon came in and dragged the people of Israel into captivity. He left us a written record—the very words of warning he delivered to them when they were engaged in defection. I want us to look carefully at this passage and read it with understanding. Then we will outline five basic attitudes that signal defection; they are as relevant as this morning's newspaper.

Doomsday Declaration

God said to Jeremiah:

> Go and proclaim in the ears of Jerusalem, saying, "Thus says
>   the LORD,
> 'I remember concerning you the devotion of your youth,
> The love of your betrothals,
> Your following after Me in the wilderness,
> Through a land not sown.
> Israel was holy to the LORD, The first of His harvest.'"
> (Jer. 2:2–3)

Here, God looks back and remembers the days of blessing and love and devotion. "Remember those early days?" God was asking. "Wasn't it great? It was like a spiritual honeymoon. Everything was fresh; everything was new. Remember those days when we loved one another? You were faithful to

Me, and I was your friend and your Father; and you walked in the path of obedience." God remembers and calls it to their attention.

But then the scene changes:

Hear the word of the LORD, O house of Jacob, and all the families of the house of Israel.
Thus says the LORD, [He's looking at the present and rebukes them]
"What injustice did your fathers find in Me,
That they went far from Me
And walked after emptiness and became empty?
And they did not say, 'Where is the LORD
Who brought us up out of the land of Egypt,
Who led us through the wilderness,
Through a land of deserts and of pits,
Through a land of drought and of deep darkness,
Through a land that no one crossed
And where no man dwelt?'
And I brought you into the fruitful land,
To eat its fruit and its good things.
But you came and defiled My land,
And My inheritance you made an abomination.
The priests did not say, 'Where is the LORD?'
And those who handle the law did not know Me;
The rulers also transgressed against Me,
And the prophets prophesied by Baal
And walked after things that did not profit.
[Not only did the people defect, but even the prophets, the priests, the preachers, and the politicians turned against God.]" (Jer. 2:4–8)

"What happened, Judah? Those days in the past were filled with blessing and delight—we walked and loved together. It's different now. You're not the same. I gave you a land that flows with milk and honey, and you perverted things and ignored Me. I haven't changed—*you* have! Where are My spokesmen?" Then comes the warning:

"But now what are you doing on the road to Egypt,
To drink the waters of the Nile?
Or what are you doing on the road to Assyria,
To drink the waters of the Euphrates? [You're on the wrong
        road! I'm warning you: you've defected.]
Your own wickedness will correct you,
And your apostasies will reprove you;
Know therefore and see that it is evil and bitter
For you to forsake the LORD your God." (Jer. 2:18–19)

These are sharp words, but they are a perfect description of a defector. These same steps those ancient Jews took are the ones every defector takes. They apply to you if you are on the verge of, or are now involved in, turning from the faith. Let's get specifics painfully specific. What are some of the characteristics of defection?

Five Signposts of Defection

1. Defection does not occur suddenly.
As Jeremiah addressed these people of God, the Jews, he reminded them that they had wandered from the way—not suddenly, but following the path of their fathers.

184

Thus says the LORD,
"What injustice did your fathers find in Me,
That they went far from Me
And walked after emptiness and became empty? . . .
And I brought you into the fruitful land,
To eat its fruit and its good things.
But you came and defiled My land,
And My inheritance you made an abomination." (Jer. 2:5, 7)

Note the progression here. The fathers began the sin, and the children carried it on. No person *suddenly* becomes base. There is no such thing as "instant defection." Erosion takes place over a period of time. One little compromise is followed by a second, and both are tolerated with a still larger compromise. Defection often begins in the thought life and then makes its way down into the heart (deep down where gutsy decisions are made, where convictions are formed) and then into the actions of life. But it takes *time* for defection to run its course.

These people did not suddenly fall prey to the enemy. The seeds of defection were sown years before the harvest was reaped.

If you are tolerating immoral things in your life, if you are compromising with thoughts that have no business being there—whether on a trip out of town, or in the secret place of your home in the evening, or in your apartment, or in the car where you drive from day to day, or from the stuff you read, or in the entertainment you seek—if the things you are prompting in your life are not God-like, then *seeds of defection are being sown*. Listen to me! They must be removed; they must be plowed up.

I've lived long enough and dealt with enough people who have allowed those seeds to blossom to know that *they never get better.* They only get worse. A compromise today will lead to a character trait tomorrow, and a character trait tomorrow will determine your future. I say to you: Uproot the seed *now.*

In his first letter to the Thessalonians, Paul wrote, "Abstain from every [appearance of] evil" (1 Thess. 5:22). Even if it *looks* wrong, get away from it. People who compromise and begin to defect tend to tolerate what is evil.

And remember, it's never big at the beginning. Roads leading to defection aren't well marked with huge warning flags. They are smooth, attractive, and appealing. The enemy is too smart to offer you enormous and obvious chunks of bait (remember chapter 7). He takes his time. Defection never occurs quickly.

2. Defection most often takes place in times of blessing.

> "And I brought you into the fruitful land,
> To eat its fruit and its good things.
> But you came and defiled My land,
> And My inheritance you made an abomination." (Jer. 2:7)

Defection most often comes in times of blessing and prosperity, not in times of trial.

Do you know when David sinned? At the zenith of his career. David's life could be charted like a housetop roof—up and then down. He had gone from being a shepherd boy to being the king of Israel. The people loved him; they lauded him with praise. He had never lost on the battlefield. He had expanded the kingdom of Israel to unbelievable heights.

And in this time of prosperity, David plunged to his ruin.

When testings come, we are purified; but when prosperity comes, we're vulnerable. Remember that!

Think of those men of Scripture who failed the Lord. On the heels of the greatest revival in history, Jonah defected. Elijah begged God to take his life only hours after he had come down from Mount Carmel, where he had reached great popularity and power in the eyes of the people. *Our most vulnerable moment is when we are enjoying times of prosperity.* God gave the children of Israel the fruit of the land to eat, and they defiled it and made it an abomination.

Warning: When you are making top grades in school, you're most vulnerable. When your family seems the closest and the strongest, you're most vulnerable. When your business has reached a level you never dreamed possible, that's a vulnerable state. Fellow pastor, when you are enjoying God's blessings and the church is growing and your fame is spreading, you're vulnerable. Be on guard! That is when things like boredom and complacency set in.

If you have served in the military, you know that the most vulnerable time for an attack is right after a battle has been won. The tendency is to sit down to a feast and take it easy. I was taught during my days in the Marine Corps that the correct maneuver immediately following victory is to set up a "hasty defense." You instantly establish communications with your forces in order to handle that early period of victory. It's tougher to remain victorious than it is to *become* victorious!

3. Defection flourishes under loose leadership.
Jeremiah pointed out the people's leaders. First he mentioned the priests. "The priests did not say, 'Where is the Lord?'" When

the people came to worship and to bring their sacrifices, the priests didn't say, "How are you and the Lord getting along?" The priests didn't talk of the Lord. There was no sense of spiritual accountability.

"And those who handle the law did not know Me." There was a trained class of professionals, called scribes, who copied the Scripture, and they didn't even know the Lord. They were going through the rituals of a professional religion.

The prophets and even the rulers "transgressed against Me . . . the prophets prophesied by Baal and walked after things that did not profit."

I have said elsewhere in this book that you never will find a perfect church. Only in that grand assembly in the heavenlies, where the "righteous men made perfect" meet around the throne of God, does perfect worship and order exist.

While I believe that weak leadership is better than no leadership, I must warn you: Be incredibly careful if you are in a church with spiritually weak leadership. Personally, I believe there is a doctrinal line you should draw.

I have only admiration for those who remain strong and active in a sleepy church and who try to wake her up. But if you are under a pastor who has trouble believing in the Trinity and is questioning the deity of Christ, the inspiration and authority of the Holy Scriptures, the return of the Lord Jesus to establish His kingdom, and other cardinal doctrines of the faith, you need to seriously consider finding another church home. You yourself could be swept away into fossilized unbelief. Unless you are an extremely discerning and strong individual, you could begin to defect without even realizing it.

From my understanding of church history (and I believe this is also true in biblical history), it is almost without exception the shepherds who err first, and then the sheep. I am talking here not about isolated, individual sin, but instead the slipping of a church or churches. Leaders set the pace.

Who did the apostle John chastise in his letters to the seven churches? The *leaders* of those churches. All the people were called upon to repent, but it was the leaders who were specifically called to account. Those seven letters were addressed to the shepherds, the messengers. Even as early as the fourth century, John Chrysostom (literally *goldenmouth,* perhaps the greatest preacher the church has ever known) said, "The road to hell is paved with the bones of errant priests." As the shepherd goes, so go the sheep.

Pastors, I beg you in the name of our Lord Jesus Christ to preach the historical, biblical gospel! Stand firm in the center of the orthodox faith and remain alive in the Spirit, serving the Lord. There is no reason to believe that being doctrinally sound is synonymous with being dull and irrelevant. If you are having problems in your faith, in your home, in your private life, go to a fellow pastor whom you know to be a man of God and submit to his help in getting you right with the Lord again.

Fellow pastors, the Scriptures warn us that we will face severe judgment as spokesmen for God. Just as eye has not seen and ear has not heard the good things God has for those who love Him, I do not believe we can begin to imagine the horror, the judgment for those ministers of the gospel who do not know and follow Christ and who lead sheep astray. God help us to be *faithful* men!

Poor leadership causes defection from Christ. Unite with a church where Christ is present and where His Word is preached and obeyed.

4. Defection involves two specific sins: forsaking the true God and finding a substitute.
They are both mentioned by the Lord Himself.

> "For My people have committed two evils.
> [No. 1] They have forsaken Me,
> The fountain of living waters,
> [No. 2] To hew for themselves cisterns,
> Broken cisterns,
> That can hold no water." (Jer. 2:13)

That's eloquent! People who had once lived and loved and walked with God committed two sins: They forsook the Lord, and they replaced Him with a bogus substitute. You will notice that the Lord is called "the fountain of living waters," and they replaced Him with poor substitutes that were broken and useless—unable even to hold water. Worse than being stagnant, substitutes run dry.

Defection does that. If you are heading "down the tubes," so to speak, you are slowly but surely turning from the Lord and putting an artificial substitute in His place. You're saying, "I don't need Him and those rigid standards that are long since out of date. What I need is something that is adventuresome and new." Perhaps you are buying into the new morality (which is nothing but the old immorality with a new title). If so, you are settling for broken cisterns that hold no water. The false substitutes will "never satisfy."

In my twenty years of ministry, one major heartache has pained me more than any other: rationalization. I mention it here because it follows the dual path we're thinking about: forsaking and substituting. Truth is set aside and rejected, often brashly. As it is "explained away" and the sin that invariably follows is justified, an alternative is put in its place. That alternative is not given by God; it's man-made.

Time after time I've seen that happen—in a marriage, for example. One of the partners gets weary of the struggle and the constant conflicts. Weakened by the relentless days of disharmony, that individual walks away from the commitment *without any biblical justification for such action.*[1] But instead of being overwhelmed by guilt and under conviction by the Spirit, the defector is all smiles, seemingly happier than ever before. And in place of the marriage commitment, there is a whole new "concept," a neat (and often highly sophisticated) philosophy in its place. What's happened? Defection has run its course, thanks to rationalization. They go well together. I don't know where you are right now, but I must warn you: Broken cisterns will soon run dry. And that brings me to the fifth and final signpost of defection.

5. Your own wickedness will correct you.
Your apostasies will reprove you. Your defection will ultimately provide its own consequences. I think this is the saddest principle of all. It isn't the Lord who loses. It isn't the devil who wins; his doom is already sealed. You lose! Your own wickedness corrects you. Your own apostasies will reprove you.

I have never seen a genuinely joyful backslidden Christian in my life. Never! I've never met one who could look me straight in the eye and say, "These are the happiest years of my life." Jeremiah noted this:

"Is Israel a slave? [Tragic scene—God's chosen people living like common slaves.] . . .

The young lions have roared at him,
They have roared loudly.
And they have made his land a waste [the lions is a
    picturesque description of the evils Israel had
    embraced]. . . .
Your own wickedness will correct you,
And your apostasies will reprove you." (Jer. 2:14, 15, 19)

When you meet backslidden Christians, they slither away like snakes. "Don't corner me!" If they see you coming on one side of the street, they'll skirt to the other side to miss you. They dread the thought of meeting a victorious Christian along the way. They'll change their circle of friends. They'll get another job, do whatever they have to do to stay away from those people whose lives are a rebuke.

If you've been in a backslidden condition like I have been in my own Christian life, you know exactly what I mean.

The Antidote

Is there no hope? Must defectors live in the clutches of sin? No! The remedy is found in Jeremiah 3:12–13:

Go, and proclaim these words toward the north and say,
"Return, faithless Israel," declares the LORD;
"I will not look upon you in anger.
For I am gracious," declares the LORD;
"I will not be angry forever.
Only acknowledge your iniquity. . . ."

Do you have a pencil? Open your Bible and circle two words. In Jeremiah 3:12, circle the word "return," and in verse

13, circle the word "acknowledge." That's the remedy: *return* and *acknowledge*.

"That doesn't sound very difficult," you say.

That's right.

"God doesn't even seem angry."

That's right too. His heart is broken. You have prostituted the things you once had claimed to be precious, and God stands like a loving father, saying, "Now, come on back home. Don't wander any longer."

Haunting my mind is the most famous parable Jesus ever told—the parable of "The Wandering Lad and the Waiting Dad," better known as "The Prodigal Son." I mentioned him in the previous chapter. That kid was determined to try everything in the world to find happiness, so he defected from his home, thinking he could find everything he wanted.

But do you know where he finally found it? *Back home.* He wanted happiness and security. He couldn't find it until he came home. He wanted a place and a name in life. He wanted to be known. He wanted to experience fulfillment. He couldn't find it, except by coming back home. He wanted love. He couldn't find it away from home, so he came back.

And did his father meet him? As we saw earlier, he had been waiting, looking down the road. And when he saw his son coming toward him, he ran to him and hugged him and kissed him and said, "My son was lost, and now he is found; he's come home!" True repentance is never rejected by our Father-God. He honors it every time.

A Final Warning

Jim Conway has put his finger on a major cause for compromise in our lives. In his book, *Men in Mid-Life Crisis,* he describes the familiar dilemma of many a man.

> The man approaching mid-life has some strange and difficult times ahead of him. He may negotiate the walk along the unfamiliar top of the brick wall with little trouble, but many men in mid-life feel more like Humpty Dumpty.
>
> The mid-life crisis is a time of high risk for marriages. It's a time of possible career disruption and extramarital affairs. There is depression, anger, frustration, and rebellion. . . .
>
> It's a time when a man reaches the peak of a mountain range. He looks back over where he has come from and forward to what lies ahead. He also looks at himself and asks, "Now that I've climbed the mountain, am I any different for it? Do I feel fulfilled? Have I achieved what I wanted to achieve?"[2]

At such times, the enemy of our souls stands perilously near, ready to pounce. Questions brought on at this crisis time can easily lead to wrong answers, cynicism, and even a bold decision to "break away and live a little." Perhaps that describes you today. I warn you as a friend who cares: You may be standing right now . . . but unless something is done to counteract your mind-set, you're headed for a fall.

The Scripture says, "Therefore let him who thinks he stands take heed lest he fall" (1 Cor. 10:12).

I don't know where you stand. You may be dangerously near the place of defection. Maybe it's moral. Maybe it's financial. Maybe it's an area of integrity in your work—you've begun cheating. And you've never been caught. Perhaps you are a minister of the gospel, one who once knew the thrill of serving Christ in purity and joy. . . . But the spark is gone. Compromise has come.

I want to tell you that whatever the defection is, it's going to rise up and curse you one of these days. Satan is encouraging you to think that if you don't get caught, it is all right. My friend, you *are* caught. Are you compromising in the faithfulness of your marriage? Are you just going through the *motions* of a happy home, while on the side you have someone who gives you quick pleasure outside of wedlock? That's sin. Adultery.

I want you to *acknowledge* the wrong and *return* to the Lord. I warn you: You'd better return. If you don't, disaster is ahead. Right this moment in your heart of hearts, I'm asking you to confess your sins, one by one, to God. Lay it all out before Him. Not until you come to terms with the whole story of your defection can you ever expect to be clean, free, and useful again in His service.

Acknowledge your present status.

Turn around.

Return to the Lord Jesus Christ.

Do it now!

Epilogue:
Some Final Reflections on Persevering

Talk about being forced to practice what I preach! This entire book on persevering through pressure was written during the remodeling of our house in California. There were chapters written in places you'd never believe . . . while I was sitting on things I'll not mention. I have been persevering through ripped-up flooring and torn-up tile, with no sink in the kitchen for two weeks, no downstairs shower for months, no table or desk to write on, and, at times, no pen to write with! Believe me, there were occasions when I was convinced some grim ghost named "Give It Up" was haunting me. At last, however, it was done. The ghost had fled. The book was finished. Hallelujah!

Perseverance paid off again. It always does.

A friend of mine, Dr. John E. Walvoord, son of the president of Dallas Seminary, had a choice experience that underscores everything I've been saying in these chapters. Back when he was a graduate student in Dallas, John heard that Dr. Victor Frankl would be delivering a series of lectures across town at Southern Methodist University. John made arrangements to spend some time with him.

Frankl was among those brave men and women who lived through the Nazi holocaust. In fact, the only reason he was not murdered with the other Jews was because he was appointed personal physician to several of the Nazi S. S. officers. What he endured is beyond description. But he persevered . . . and lived.

During the memorable conversation with this remarkable man several years ago, John still remembers a statement he made, which Frankl might call his basic philosophy of life. It went something like this:

> The reason so many people are unhappy today and seeking help to cope with life is that they fail to understand what human existence is all about. Until we recognize that life is not just something to be enjoyed but rather is a task that each of us is assigned, we'll never find meaning in our lives and we'll never be truly happy.

That may not fit in with what you've been fed since you became a Christian. In fact, it probably doesn't. It certainly doesn't square with a little motto I learned as a child: "A smile a day keeps the devil away." Nonsense. Frankl was right. *Life is a task.* A tough one. Sometimes it's absolutely unbearable.

Some days we do well just to survive . . . to say nothing of excelling. Therefore, persevering becomes essential to living—the only key that unlocks the door of hope. Through perseverance character is built, strong and solid character that brings about hope.

Frankl didn't say that, but another Jew from another era did. His name was Paul:

> We also rejoice in our sufferings, [Why?] because we know that suffering produces perseverance; perseverance, character; and character, hope. (Rom. 5:3, NIV)

Why keep persevering? Why continue standing against the strong currents of temptation, fear, anger, loss, stress, impossibilities, misunderstanding, and mistakes? Why fight defection? Why overcome inferiority? Why keep on waiting? Why? I'll tell you why. Because it is in the realistic arena that true character is forged, shaped, tempered, and polished. Because it is there that the life of Jesus Christ is given the maximum opportunity to be reproduced in us, replacing a thin, fragile internal theology with a tough, reliable set of convictions that enables us to handle life rather than escape from it.

Because life is a task, we need strength to face it, not speed to run from it. When the foundation shakes, when Christian friends—even the *leaders*—are immoral and falling into apostasy, when the bottom drops out and brutal blows attempt to pound us into the corner of doubt and unbelief, *we need what perseverance offers:* willingness to accept whatever comes, strength to face it head-on, determination to stand firm, and insight to see the Lord's hand in it all.

Without it, we stumble and fall. And God is grieved.

With it, we survive and conquer. And God is glorified.

Chapter 1

Perseverance: Archaic Word of Relevance

1. We all prefer "great and fantastic" days over "growing and learning" days, don't we? They're just simply easier, more pleasant.

But to complicate matters, we not only want great days; we think we're supposed to have them. After all, that's what being a Christian's all about. We're supposed to have overcome sin by now, and God is perfectly capable of fixing any other problem that might arise. Right?

So to make a "growing and learning" day even harder, we add to it guilt or disillusionment or bewilderment. And things go downhill from there. We can only go so long ignoring that nagging feeling that something's just a little wrong with our picture of Christianity.

Read through those Four Spiritual Flaws one more time. Do any of them bring a sheepish grin to your face—a reaction that says, "That's me!"? Do any of them come as a surprise? On another piece of paper, draw a chart. On the left side, list the four flaws, leaving space in between. On the right side, jot down the implications each one has in your life.

2. Whether you've been going to church for six months or sixty years, you've probably already learned more spiritual

truth than you could ever apply in a lifetime. Read Hebrews 5:11–14. Read it aloud if you're in a group. What does this passage tell you about the difference between growing *old* in the Lord and growing up in the Lord?

3. God is gracious enough to sprinkle a few "great and fantastic" days in among the "growing and learning" days— probably just to give us a rest and some much-needed encouragement. But it's those "growing and learning" days where the true character of Christ begins to be forged in our lives.

Read James 1:2–4. What do we gain from those difficult times, those "growing and learning" days? List the qualities they add to our lives.

Chapter 2

Misunderstanding: Paralyzing Sting of Humanity

1. Just to get in the mood for this study, shuffle through your mental scrapbook to a time when you felt misunderstood. Amazing how that memory's still a little tender to the touch, isn't it? Especially if, like the guy with the turkey, you never got a chance to set the record straight. Try to keep those feelings fresh as we continue—it'll make the message clearer and more likely to be applied!

2. If anybody knew what it was like to be on the wrong end of a misunderstanding, it was David. Few of us have had to run for our lives after an innocent—even noble—act! Look again at that pattern of development in Psalm 140. First,

there's the sense of *vulnerability* Then the report of *exaggeration* by the offended party. Next comes the *speaking aloud* of the offense.

If you've ever been misunderstood, you don't need anyone to tell you about that feeling of vulnerability. But how often have you been, not the *misunderstood* party, but the mistakenly *offended* party? Those occasions probably don't stand out in your memory quite so clearly, but try to dredge one out. Did you find yourself elaborating on the offense, building it up in your mind to—as you saw later—ridiculous proportions? When you shared your offense with someone else, did you choose someone who would correct you . . . or someone likely to take your part without any objective reasoning?

3. What is your first reaction when you've been misunderstood? If you're like most people, you feel like marching right over to say, "Now look here, I didn't mean . . . !" And sometimes that's the best approach. But sometimes you only dig your hole a little deeper.

In those situations where your explanation isn't likely to be heard or accepted, there's another way to handle it. Read Exodus 14:14 and Psalm 140:6, 9–10. What do those verses imply that you should do? Write down your answer or discuss it with your group.

4. Reread the C. S. Lewis quote on page 21. Taking the three sections one at a time, what do you think each one means? How have you seen each one to be true in your own experience?

- God whispers to us in our pleasures.
- [He] speaks in our conscience.

- [He] shouts in our pains: It is His megaphone to rouse a deaf world.

5. Sometimes a severe misunderstanding leads to resentment, which can cripple us emotionally for many years. Are you still hurting over a misunderstanding that has cost you dearly? Lewis B. Smedes has written an excellent book that shows us how to be free from the pains of our past. It's called *Forgive and Forget*.

Chapter 3

Stress: Threatening Storm of Anxiety

1. Some of the stress in our lives is as superficial as a tight collar on a thickening neck—we just need to undo a button or two. But most of it scratches below the surface, etching wrinkles on our foreheads and scraping ulcers in our stomachs. Quite often, the source of the stress is less external than internal. It comes from *hurry*, *worry*, or *bury*.

Which of those three words would you say characterizes your inner life? There may be more than one. See if you can identify the way each word contributes to the stress you are feeling.

2. In Hebrew, *trouble* means "to be restricted; to be tied up in a narrow, cramped place." Southerners say it more succinctly: "to be between a rock and a hard place." But any way you look at it, trouble just means trouble.

Is there any kind of trouble on your mind right now? How is it making you feel . . . threatened? Under attack? Maybe just worn out and depressed? Complete the activity below that fits your mood the best.

• If you're feeling threatened, you need to conquer your fear. Try looking up Isaiah 41:10; 2 Timothy 1:7; Joshua 1:9; and Psalm 27:1, 10. Then make a chart on a separate sheet of paper. On one side, list all the things those verses tell you to do—or not to do. On the other side, list all the things God promises to be or do for us. It may be eye-opening, and it will surely be reassuring.

• If you're feeling under attack you need to take charge of your tendency to just turn tail and run or to seek protection from sources that can't help.

Elvis thought that fans and finances could protect him from the stress that attacked him throughout his life. To what do you look for protection? What gives you the feeling of standing on solid, immovable ground? Complete this sentence: I will not be moved because of _____. Search your heart for the real answer. If it's anything but "the God of hope," you're fooling yourself; any other ground could crumble at any time.

• If you're feeling tired or depressed, you need to stop striving. But how many of us, down deep inside, feel good about ourselves when we're simply doing nothing? Isn't there something inside us that feels just a little more spiritual, a little more productive, when our days are filled from morning until night?

Reread the poem on pages 32–33; then take a look at your appointment book for last week—or last month, or last year. What do you wish you'd spent more time doing? Is there anything you could have spent less time doing? Or perhaps have cut out all together?

Look ahead to this week's schedule. Pick a time for doing something you enjoy . . . and write it on the schedule in ink.

3. If stress has really got you feeling like you're in a pressure cooker, ready to scream off some steam, maybe you'd like to do some further reading on this subject. Two excellent books on stress are *When I Relax I Feel Guilty* by Tim Hansel, and *Adrenaline and Stress* by Archibald D. Hart.

Chapter 4

Loss: Lonely Times of Crisis

1. There are few things in life we feel so keenly as loss. From the loss of a favorite old sweatshirt to the loss of an old, dear friend, we feel to some degree cheated, deprived. For a time we even fight the reality of the loss. We go on looking, turning out dresser drawers, hoping that what is missing will somehow miraculously turn up.

Obviously, a sweatshirt has nowhere near the importance of a person, or even a job or an opportunity. But all of us feel the desire to hold on to what we have, even the smallest things. We see them as God's gifts to us, and we feel hurt and offended, even resentful, when He tries to pry them from our lives.

Read Job 2:10 again. How does your view of a good, loving God square with the idea of a God who also brings adversity?

Using your concordance, look up verses dealing with adversity and blessing. If this is a dichotomy you have trouble reconciling, why not make a study of it?

2. When a major loss comes into our lives, it doesn't usually tap us quietly on the shoulder. Instead, it comes barreling in through the front door, demanding our immediate attention.

When that happens, it's sometimes easy to overlook that light, insistent tapping on the patio door. The tapping that announces the arrival of a big present in a little box, a new quality of character that will see us through the flood of tears and help us emerge a stronger person rather than a diminished one.

Is there loss in your life right now? Have you been so busy with your unpleasant visitor, so attuned to the sounds of sorrow, that you've missed that backdoor knock?

You can't ignore your grief. But that little plain-wrapped package on the back steps of your heart could contain the hope that you need to persevere. Won't you untie its strings?

3. The most difficult thing to bear about loss can be the terrifying feeling that, in your moment of greatest need, God has abandoned you. Have you experienced that feeling and the anguish that accompanies it? Sometimes the only way to fight those feelings is with facts. Even though we know God is sometimes wrathful, sometimes angry, sometimes severe, in His heart of hearts, He is also compassionate. He longs to heal our wounds and tenderly touch us with His mercy. If it's reassurance of that nature that you need now, read the following passages of Scripture and let their comfort soothe your aching soul.

Job 5:8–11
Psalm 23
Psalm 55:22
Matthew 5:4
John 16:33
2 Corinthians 1:3–5

Chapter 5

Impossibilities: Uncrossable Rivers of Life

1. Life isn't easy for any of us. It's one long series of uphill climbs followed by a few downhill slides, and in between are a lot of long, hot, dusty stretches of road.

But every once in a while, just when we've crossed the highest mountain, we come around a bend and find ourselves facing the widest, wildest, swiftest river we've ever seen . . . and not a bridge or a boat in sight.

That's an impossibility. And maybe that's where you're standing right now.

What are the swells in that river made up of? When you stare into its roiling, rocky depths, what do you see? A dead-end career . . . a rebellious child . . . a hopeless marriage? You fill in the blank. And keep a picture of it tucked in the back of your mind as you turn your focus to God in this study.

2. You've probably known the story of the loaves and the fishes since Vacation Bible School days. But how well do you know two of the main characters?

Take out your Bible and read the story again; you'll find it in John 6. Pay special attention to Philip and Andrew. Remember, Philip's the one who saw the size of the problem and forgot about the size of God; Andrew's the pessimist who figured the odds were against them. Which of those characters reminds you of yourself? Why?

In your impossible situation, is it time to put down your calculator, to shelve your doubts . . . to just take your hands off and simply pray?

3. Did you do what you were supposed to at the end of this chapter? If not, here's your second chance.

Copy the following statement on an index card. Then read it aloud, over and over again, until you have it memorized. After that? Put it where you'll see it! Then you won't forget you already know it.

We are all faced with a series of great opportunities brilliantly disguised as impossible situations.

Chapter 6

Waiting: Lingering Test of Patience

1. Maybe one of the reasons we hate waiting is that it feels so inactive and unproductive. The very word conjures up images of a doctor's office lobby with uncomfortable chairs, dated magazines, and nothing to do but twiddle our thumbs.

But did you catch the definition of *wait* as it's used in Isaiah 40:31? It means "to twist or to stretch in order to become strong." Hardly the picture of inactivity! It's more like strenuous exercise, taking your little thread of hope and winding it round and round God's unbreakable steel cable of reliability.

Are you twiddling your thumbs when you ought to be twisting rope? Are you willing to start expending some energy? If so, take a few minutes to outline what "twisting rope" might mean for you.

2. What are you in a hurry for right now—a job to open up, a husband to come on the scene? The list of possibilities is endless. But whatever it is, the right resolution will be like a

succulent purple grape, ripe and satisfying. Before you taste it, though, you may have to take time to pick out some bitter seeds. And when your fingers start getting messy, you may be tempted to settle for a bunch of seedless green grapes that you can just pop into your mouth.

What's the purple grape just out of your reach? Are you willing to wait for it? Are there any green grapes within view, making your mouth water and your stomach growl? Take time now to prayerfully identify them, and to set your sights on what you—and God—know is best.

3. Waiting feels like a test of our patience, and it is. But it's mentioned so often in Scripture that it seems to be even more than that. How do you think God views waiting? Why do you think He allows that process in our lives? Make a study of the following verses before you answer those questions.

Psalm 27:5; 37:9; 40:1
Isaiah 30:18; 40:31
Romans 8:25

Chapter 7

Temptation: Vulnerable Flaw of Weakness

1. Temptation is inevitable; not a one of us is immune. But temptation is also individual. The thing that sets your mouth watering and your heart pounding may not even capture the attention of someone else.

What captures your eye and draws you irresistibly toward it? Before we go any further, identify to yourself that one thing Satan can usually count on to lure you away from right-eousness.

2. Take out your Bible and read Matthew 4:1–11. In this passage, you'll see Jesus Himself facing temptation in all three of the areas we usually face it in: physical gratification, power, and material gain.

How did Jesus respond to Satan's bait? Why do you think Jesus chose that method?

Was His method for handling temptation any different from your own? In what way?

3. We saw from the story of Joseph and Potiphar's wife that sometimes the best way to deal with temptation is to simply run the other way. But our natural tendency is to tiptoe toward it, to see how close we can get before we actually give in.

Have you built your life too near a danger zone? If so, describe it. What kind of cracks and warped floors have you begun to notice around the building of your morals?

Maybe it's time to pack up and move away.

4. Be honest with yourself on this question: Don't you sometimes feel more like the victim of a tempting situation than someone who has deliberately sinned? Don't temptations sometimes just seem too strong to resist?

It's a common feeling, but is it accurate? Read 1 Corinthians 10:13, preferably from *The Living Bible*, before you answer.

How does that verse impact your view of temptation? Does it offer any comfort or sources of strength?

You may have noticed as you studied Jesus' temptations that He retorted to Satan using Scripture. Wouldn't 1 Corinthians

10:13 be a good verse to have in your own arsenal when Satan starts trying to convince you of your weakness toward certain things?

Write this verse down on a sheet of paper and copy it several times. When you can write it without looking back to the original, you have learned it. To prove it to yourself, say it at least one time out loud. This is one verse that bears repeating!

Chapter 8

Mistakes: Inevitable Marks of Imperfection

1. You know how it feels when you realize you've made a mistake—especially a big one. There's that awful sinking feeling in the pit of your stomach and the flush that comes to your cheeks. And more often than not, the desire to avoid everyone who might have seen you make it.

Sometimes it's because we're too embarrassed to face what we've done; sometimes it's because we have too much pride to admit we were wrong. And sometimes it's because we fear we won't be understood, that we'll be rejected.

It's a legitimate fear when you're dealing with human beings—but not when you're dealing with the Lord!

Look up the following verses. What do they have to say about God's reaction to us, mistakes and all?

Hebrews 4:15
Psalm 31:8
Psalm 103:13
2 Samuel 24:14
Ephesians 2:4–5

2. Mistakes and sins are two different things, but they do have one thing in common—natural consequences. For that reason, if for no other, it pays to catch them before you make them! Wherever possible anyway.

Just as we get in a rut with the kinds of temptation we respond to, so we follow a well-worn path toward the same kinds of mistakes, again and again and again.

Review the five kinds of mistakes we studied in this chapter: *panic-prompted mistakes, good-intentioned mistakes, negligent mistakes, unrestrained-curiosity mistakes, and blind-spot mistakes.* Which kind bears a sign with your name on it? If you look back over some of your past mistakes, do you see a pattern emerging? Ask someone who knows you well to help you pinpoint where you usually go astray. Then make plans to head the other way the next time that fork in the road appears.

3. You know by now that God has forgiven you for the mistakes you have made, even the foolish and costly ones. But you may not have forgiven yourself. Have you read *Healing Grace* by David A. Seamands? It may be just what you need to help release yourself from the terrible grip of guilt.

Chapter 9

Inferiority: Contagious Plague of Self-Doubt

1. If we decided to, any one of us could develop an inferiority complex, just by focusing on our faults. It doesn't take more than ten minutes to ruin your whole afternoon that way. You know that because you've done it to yourself any number of times.

During those times of critical self-appraisal, we forget that feelings of inferiority have very little to do with actual inadequacy—and everything to do with what we choose to think about.

Today, let's be realistic about ourselves—but for once, not focus on our failings. First, we'll get a scriptural view of ourselves, and then we'll look at a more personal one.

Look up the following passages and write down what each verse has to say about you.

Matthew 6:25–30
Ephesians 2:10
Philippians 1:6; 2:13
Romans 8:29
Zephaniah 3:17

Now take an inventory of your specific attributes, writing them down as you go. Don't stop until you've listed at least twenty!

2. The personality and skills of the people up front can easily make those of us in the pew feel as though we have little to offer. But if the truth were known, those in the pulpit would find it almost impossible to contribute the things God designed us to give.

Read through 1 Corinthians 12:14–25. If you compared yourself to a part of a physical body, which part would you say you resemble? In function, that is—not in actual fact! Describe the uses for that part of the physical body, and compare them to the ways you are useful to the body of Christ.

3. If you consistently struggle with feelings of self-doubt, get hold of a copy of *Self Talk: Key to Personal Growth* by Dr. David Stoop. It's an invaluable resource that will open the door to some practical changes.

Chapter 10

Fear: Fierce Grip of Panic

1. Denis Waitley, in his book *Seeds of Greatness,* defines fear this way.

*F*alse
*E*ducation
*A*ppearing
*R*eal[1]

Many of our fears are a result of things we've come to believe that aren't necessarily true. For instance, a shy person may be afraid of meeting new people because he wrongly assumes people in general don't like him. A bright, well-educated woman might be afraid to apply for an appealing new job because she doesn't believe she has anything to offer.

Those fears can have their roots in all kinds of harmful soils; oftentimes, their seeds were planted back in childhood, through less-than-positive parenting or encounters with less-than-sensitive peers.

Ongoing fears like those may need to be addressed at a deeper level than we can reach in this brief study. But one false belief that many of us have is that, in whatever our particular fears, we are alone.

That's exactly what Satan would like us to believe, whether we're facing the malicious point of an assailant's knife or a new experience, we're not sure we're ready for. But take a moment, won't you, to look up Hebrews 13:5–6.

The word translated as *never* in verse 5 is stronger than the English can make it. The sentence would better read: "I will never, no never, no never leave you or forsake you." Strong promise, isn't it? It's a helpful one to remember when we feel fear's clammy breath sending chills down our spine. So that this passage will be a ready source of courage in the moment you most need it, commit it to memory before you turn the next page.

Chapter 11

Anger: Burning Fuse of Hostility

Anger . . . it's such a common emotion, one even Jesus felt. We probably all experience it in at least a mild form every day. When we get trapped on the freeway behind a slow-moving truck. When we're billed a third time for a magazine we never subscribed to. When the neighbor's dog tears up the flower bed.

But even though it's such a common emotion, it's one we Christians have a hard time dealing with—some of us because we can't control our anger and feel too ashamed to ask for help; others, because we're too uncomfortable with it to allow ourselves to recognize it when it comes.

Choose the exercise below which best suits your needs in this area.

1. If you have trouble controlling your temper, it may be

because you're not sure exactly how or when to react to anger-inciting incidents. Many Christians are afraid to see what the Bible has to say about this subject because they feel sure its words would condemn them. But you may be surprised to find some practical advice from Someone who really understands how you feel.

Why not give God's Word a chance to help you temper your temperament? You might want to study in more depth the passages from our chapter, or you can use a concordance to see what others are available. Whichever you choose, make a chart on another sheet of paper and fill it in as you read. On one side, list the verses you study. On the other side, jot down the advice they give.

2. Are you one of those people who seems to never feel angry—who meets every irritation with a forgiving shrug and a "let's move on" smile? Congratulations! You've done a great job of mastering self-control. But you've also done yourself a great disservice in smothering your God-given emotions, and that will eventually produce unhealthy results.

Maybe you've been uncomfortably aware that if your smooth exterior gets a little bit ruffled, your anger seems to skyrocket way past appropriate levels. A spilled glass of milk brings on white-knuckled fury; an inconsiderate clerk causes unwarranted rage. If that sounds like you, it's likely you have a reservoir of stagnant irritations, and they're beginning to spill over the dam.

If you recognized yourself in the descriptions above, there's good news—you can relax your rigid self-standards for squelching anger. In fact, God says anger is okay! To gain some perspective on how to drain the reservoir without flooding your friends and family, see Neil Clark Warren's book *Make Anger Your Ally.*

Chapter 12

Defection: Final Stage of Compromise

1. Do you remember when you first became a Christian? If you were too young for it to be a clear memory, think back to the time when you first felt the excitement of Christ's presence in your life. Remember the zeal with which you witnessed, the commitment with which you approached your quiet time and your responsibilities at church?

It's hard to maintain that enthusiasm for long; in fact much of the Christian walk is choosing to plod along once that initial excitement has gone.

It's all too easy, though, for that walk of faith to become a walk of defection. Sometimes it happens so gradually we don't even notice.

Maybe it's time to examine the path you're on. Is it still straight and smooth, paved with the stones of righteousness? Do you keep it swept clean from dirty thoughts and the debris of sin? Or has it become a little rough in places, with wide spots in the road to allow for detours? Are you getting a little careless about staying on course? It doesn't take much time on a side road to lose sight of your destination.

What is it that you're really aiming for in life? When you look down the road a piece, what kind of person do you want to see? Write out a description of your spiritual goals for the next year. It will help you realign your focus.

2. As we discovered in this chapter, defection rarely happens overnight or as a result of one major incident. Rather, it's a slow process of little compromises that add up to one big change of heart.

Can you think of any small compromises you've been making in your life lately? Maybe you've let your standards slip a little in the area of the sensual, or maybe you've hedged a bit in your work ethics. Perhaps you're not spending as much time with your family as you planned to, or you've loosened your ideals when it comes to the type of videos or television programs you allow in your home.

Consider this issue carefully. Do any of your standards need straightening up? Pick one or two main areas and take time now to write out some new resolves.

Epilogue

Some Final Reflections on Persevering

1. Remember those Four Spiritual Flaws we read about in Chapter 1? After a whole book on the problems people—even Christians—face, it's clear why they're called Flaws instead of Laws! But those beliefs can be so subtly and strongly woven into our lives that they deserve one final look.

Read again the Frankl quote on page 200, and compare it to the Four Spiritual Flaws. What are the differences between those two approaches to life?

Do you agree with Frankl that life is a task? In what way or ways is that true? How can looking at life as a task make life more meaningful and happy?

2. Let's look again at the statement made by another Jew who knew what it was to suffer and persevere. We find it in Romans 5:3. "We also rejoice in our sufferings, because we know that suffering produces perseverance; perseverance, character; and character, hope" (NIV). Paraphrase this verse to make it more personally meaningful. Instead of using *we*, use *I* And instead of using the general words *sufferings* and *suffering*, fill in the specific trial that you are suffering right now.

Chapter 2

1. C. S. Lewis, *The Problem of Pain* (New York: Macmillan, 1971), 93.

Chapter 3

1. Judith Viorst, *Alexander and the Terrible, Horrible, No Good, Very Bad Day* (Hartford, Conn.: Connecticut Printers, 1972), 1, 23.

2. Ibid.

3. Thomas V. Bonoma and Dennis P. Slevin, *Executive Survival Manual* (Boston: CBI Publishing Company, 1978) 58–59.

4. Reprinted from Tim Hansel, *When I Relax I Feel Guilty* (Elgin, Ill.: David C. Cook Publishing Co., 1979). Used by permission.

5. Ibid., 44–45.

6. Stuart Briscoe, *What Works When Life Doesn't* (Wheaton, Ill.: Victor Books, 1976), 125.

Chapter 4

1. Joseph Bayly, *The View from a Hearse* (Elgin, Ill.: David C. Cook, 1973), 12.

2. Joyce Landorf, *Mourning Song* (Old Tappan, N.J.: Fleming H. Revell, 1974), 52–53.

3. Meredith Kline, *The Wycliffe Bible Commentary*, Charles F. Pfeiffer, ed. (Chicago: Moody Press, 1962), 463.

4. Bayly, *The View from a Hearse*, 40–41.

Chapter 5

1. "Got Any Rivers," © copyright 1945. Renewal 1973 by Oscar Eliason. Assigned to Singspiration, Inc. All rights reserved. Used by permission.

2. Mary A Thomson, "O Zion, Haste," *Worship and Service Hymnal* (Chicago: Hope Publishing Co., 1966), 430.

3. Howard G. Hendricks, *Say It with Love* (Wheaton, Ill.: Victor Books, 1973), 91–92.

Chapter 6

1. "Speak, Lord in the Stillness," © copyright 1951 by Singspirations, Inc. All rights reserved. Used by permission.

Chapter 7

1. Dag Hammarskjold, *Markings* (New York: Alfred A. Knopf, 1964), 15.

2. Dietrich Bonhoeffer, *Temptation* (London: SCM Press, 1964), 33.

Chapter 8

1. Benjamin Franklin, Maxims prefixed to *Poor Richard's Almanac* [1757], reprinted in *Familiar Quotations,* John Bartlett, ed. (Boston: Little, Brown and Company, 1955), 330.

2. Mark Twain, *Pudd'nhead Wilson's New Calendar,* Ch. 30. reprinted in *Familiar Quotations,* John Bartlett, ed., p. 679.

Chapter 9

1. James Dobson, *Hide or Seek* (Old Tappan, N.J.: Fleming H. Revell, 1974), 133.

2. Ibid. 134.

Chapter 10

1. Wayne W. Dyer, *Your Erroneous Zones* (New York: Avon, 1976), 97–124.

2. Ruth Harms Calkin, *Tell Me Again, Lord, I Forget* (Elgin, Ill.: David C. Cook, 1974).

3. Ruth Harms Calkin, *Lord, You Love to Say Yes* (Elgin, Ill.: David C. Cook 1976).

Chapter 11

1. Thomas Jefferson, *A Decalogue of Canons for Observation in Practical Life* (Feb. 21, 1825), reprinted in *Familiar Quotations*, John Bartlett, ed., 376.

2. Mark Twain, *Pudd'nhead Wilson's Calendar*, Ch. 3, *Familiar Quotations*, John Bartlett, ed. 678.

3. This topic is discussed at length in my book *You and Your Child* (Nashville: Thomas Nelson, 1977).

4. Washington Irving, *The Sketch-Book* (1819–1820), reprinted in *Familiar Quotations*, John Bartlett, ed., 446.

5. David Augsburger, *Caring Enough to Confront* (Glendale, Calif.: Regal Books, 1973).

Chapter 12

1. *Note:* Having searched the Scriptures for many years on the subject of divorce and remarriage, I have come to the conclusion that divorce and remarriage are permissible in two situations.

First, if a partner is guilty of sexual immorality and willfully refuses to live faithfully with his or her spouse, the faithful mate has the option to leave and marry another (Matt. 19:3–9).

Second, if a Christian is married to a non-Christian and the unbelieving partner leaves (deserts, abandons the Christian mate, wants nothing to do with the marriage any longer), the deserted believer has the option to leave and marry another (1 Cor. 7: 12–15).

In both cases it is ideal (if the offended partner can forgive and persevere) to remain and make the marriage work through God's grace and power. There are occasions, however, when that simply cannot happen. My point regarding rationalization has to do with breaking a marriage partnership without actual biblical grounds for such action.

2. Jim Conway, *Men in Mid-Life Crisis* (Elgin, Ill.: David C. Cook, 1978), 17.

Study Guide

1. Denis Waitley, *Seeds of Greatness* (Old Tappan, N.J.: Fleming H. Revell Co., 1983), 34.